Introduction to One Digital Identity

Strategies, Innovations, and Future Trends

Shivakumar R. Goniwada

Apress®

Introduction to One Digital Identity: Strategies, Innovations, and Future Trends

Shivakumar R. Goniwada
Gubbalala, Bangalore, Karnataka, India

ISBN-13 (pbk): 979-8-8688-0254-6
https://doi.org/10.1007/979-8-8688-0255-3

ISBN-13 (electronic): 979-8-8688-0255-3

Managing Director, Apress Media LLC: Welmoed Spahr
Acquisitions Editor: Celestin Suresh John
Development Editor: James Markham
Editorial Assistant: Gryffin Winkler

Cover designed by eStudioCalamar

Cover image designed by pikisuperstar on freepik (freepik.com)

Distributed to the book trade worldwide by Springer Science+Business Media New York, 1 New York Plaza, Suite 4600, New York, NY 10004-1562, USA. Phone 1-800-SPRINGER, fax (201) 348-4505, e-mail orders-ny@springer-sbm.com, or visit www.springeronline.com. Apress Media, LLC is a California LLC and the sole member (owner) is Springer Science + Business Media Finance Inc (SSBM Finance Inc). SSBM Finance Inc is a **Delaware** corporation.

For information on translations, please e-mail booktranslations@springernature.com; for reprint, paperback, or audio rights, please e-mail bookpermissions@springernature.com.

Apress titles may be purchased in bulk for academic, corporate, or promotional use. eBook versions and licenses are also available for most titles. For more information, reference our Print and eBook Bulk Sales web page at http://www.apress.com/bulk-sales.

Any source code or other supplementary material referenced by the author in this book is available to readers on GitHub. For more detailed information, please visit https://www.apress.com/gp/services/source-code.

Paper in this product is recyclable

This book is dedicated to those who may need access to the resources and opportunities many take for granted. May this book serve as a reminder that knowledge and learning are powerful tools that can transform lives and create new opportunities for those who seek them.

Table of Contents

About the Author

Shivakumar R. Goniwada is a renowned author, inventor, and technology leader with more than 24 years of experience in architecting cutting-edge cloud-native, data analytics, and event-driven systems. He currently is a chief enterprise architect at Accenture, where he leads a team of highly skilled technology enterprise and cloud architects. Throughout his career, Shivakumar has successfully led numerous complex projects across various industries and geographical locations. His expertise has earned him 10 software patents in areas such as cloud computing, polyglot architecture, software engineering, and the Internet of Things. He is a sought-after speaker at global conferences and has made significant contributions to the field through his publications. Shivakumar has a master's degree in technology architecture and certifications in Google Professional, AWS, and data science. He also completed an executive MBA at the prestigious MIT Sloan School of Management. His notable books include *Cloud-Native Architecture and Design* and *Introduction to Datafication*, both published by Apress.

About the Technical Reviewer

 **Sudhir Sid** is an enterprise security leader with more than 18 years of IT security experience leading organizations in the implementation of IAM processes and products. Mr. Sid specializes as a cybersecurity expert participating in the strategy, planning, design, development, and implementation of business and IT architectures including cloud, security, web, and mobile architectures in large to small enterprises.

He has broad experience across the cybersecurity domain and has helped deliver complex implementations on digital identity access and management, identity governance, privileged access management, and other cybersecurity domains.

He is a certified AWS Cloud Security Architect and Certified AWS Solutions Architect and has strong knowledge and experience with many of the leading cybersecurity products/companies such as SailPoint, Cyberark, Okta, Broadcom Identity Suite, Micro Focus, NetIQ, PingFederate, and PingDirectory.

Mr. Sid currently works as an associate director at Guidehouse, a leading global provider of consulting services in the public sector and commercial markets, with broad capabilities in management, technology, and risk consulting.

Acknowledgments

Many thanks to my mother, S. Jayamma, and late father, G.M. Rudrappa, who taught me the value of hard work, and to my wife Nirmala and daughter, Neeharika, without whom I wouldn't have been able to work long hours into the night every day of the week. Finally, I'd like to thank my friends and colleagues, as well as the mentors at Mphasis, Accenture, and other corporations who have guided me throughout my career.

Thank you also to Celestin Suresh John, Shobana Srinivasan, Gryffin Winkler, and the other Apress team members for allowing me to work with you and Apress, and to all who have helped this book become a reality. Thank you to my mentors, Bert Hooyman and Abubacker Mohamed, for guiding me in the right direction.

Introduction

"Identity will be the most valuable commodity for citizens in the future, and it will exist primarily online."

—Eric Schmidt

As we navigate through an era increasingly dominated by online interactions, the need for a unified, secure, and universally accepted digital identity has become more apparent than ever.

The book sets the stage for a comprehensive exploration of how such a singular digital identity can be conceptualized, developed, and implemented across various platforms and services. It delves into the challenges and opportunities presented by the current fragmented digital identity landscape, where individuals often juggle multiple usernames, passwords, and profiles across different digital domains, and it proposes a paradigm shift toward a singular, self-sovereign identity that users control entirely. The book also unpacks the mechanics of decentralized identifiers (DIDs), elucidating how this technology leverages blockchain technology to create secure, portable, and universally recognizable identities.

The book then transitions to the practical implications of implementing a "one digital identity" system by covering details such as the technical infrastructure, the regulatory hurdles to navigate, and the societal impacts of such a shift. The book addresses the challenges and considerations inherent in transitioning to a DID-based digital identity system, including interoperability and scalability among the different blockchain platforms. We further discuss the importance of developing a supportive ecosystem that includes regulatory bodies, technology providers, and end users, highlighting collaboration as the key to the widespread adoption of DIDs.

Whether you are a student, analyst, engineer, technologist, part of the C-suite, or someone simply interested in the world of digital identity, this book will provide you with comprehensive coverage of DIDs, regulatory details, and implementation details.

CHAPTER 1

Redefining Digital Identity In New Era

Our virtual and physical lives are increasingly linked to the multiple apps, services, and devices we use to access various experiences. The digital world allows you to interact with hundreds of companies, and collaboration with various people has become complicated. Because of this complexity, identity data has often been exposed to security breaches, and these breaches impact our day-to-day life. In this situation, we as users have the right to create an identity that we own, control, and store securely.

The concept of *one digital identity* means individuals have a unified and seamless identity across multiple platforms, services, borders, etc. Having one digital identity simplifies authentication and authorization across access platforms. With one digital identity, users can log in once and access all their related and authorized applications.

In this chapter, you will learn the following:

- What a digital identity is
- How digital identities have evolved
- Why we need a digital identity
- The importance of one digital identity in the modern age
- Types of digital identities
- Data privacy and regulations around digital identities

Understanding Digital Identities

A *digital identity* represents a person, organization, or device in the digital realm and encompasses various attributes, credentials, and data that define that entity online.

1

© Shivakumar R. Goniwada 2024
S. R. Goniwada, *Introduction to One Digital Identity*, https://doi.org/10.1007/979-8-8688-0255-3_1

The Evolution of Digital Identities

In the early days of the Internet, digital identity was a concept yet to be realized. People lived their lives without much thought about their online presence or the need for a secure and unified identity across digital platforms. However, as technology continued to advance and the Internet became an integral part of our daily lives, the concept of digital identities began to evolve.

In those early days, people used a simple username and password to access various online services. There was little concern for privacy or security, and people freely shared personal information online. I can call this a "time of innocence," but it was a stepping stone to future challenges.

As the Internet grew and especially as social media platforms emerged, people began creating more detailed online profiles, sharing real names, profile pictures, and personal interests and addresses openly. Digital identities become intertwined with one's social life, and the concept of managing an online persona gained importance. At the same time, cybercrime, theft, and misuse of information also increased. The simplistic username and password system proved vulnerable to hackers and malicious actors. In fact, many high-profile data breaches have exposed millions of users' private information over the years.

As a result, the industry worked on bolstering security. Two-factor authentication (2FS) and multifactor authentication (MFA) emerged as popular solutions. With this technology, users must provide an additional piece of information or use a secondary trusted device to log in. Biometric authentication gained attention along with MFA, allowing people to use their fingerprints, facial recognition, eye scanners, etc., to verify their login credentials.

The concern over data privacy and centralized control increased, and a new concept arrived called *self-sovereign identity* (SSI). Although still in the evaluation stage, an SSI will give individuals full control over their digital identity, storing personal information securely on their devices or in decentralized systems in the blockchain. The *blockchain* is a distributed ledger technology known for its decentralized and secure nature. It's essentially a sequence of records, each containing a list of transactions. Once a record (or *block*) is completed, it's added to the sequence (or *chain*) in a linear and chronological order. Each block is linked to the previous one, creating a secure and unalterable record of transactions. This solution provides users with a data custodian, who shares only the necessary information with trusted parties. The blockchain plays a significant role in shaping the evolution of digital identities with decentralized identifiers (DIDs), which allow for more secure and privacy-focused identification methods. You do not need to rely solely on centralized authorities for verification.

Along with DIDs, digital wallets have become a prominent feature in the evolution of digital identities. These wallets store personal identification data, making them essential to an individual's online identity. Examples of digital wallets are India's DigiLocker and password-less technologies such as YubiKey. You can store all your personal details, such as driver licenses, certificates, insurance etc., in these tools.

Artificial intelligence (AI) plays a significant role in identity verification processes. Identity verification is used in many companies in Europe and the United States, and identity verification platforms such as iDenfy provides facial recognition, 3D liveness detection and authentication, etc. AI algorithms enable robust and accurate identity checks using facial recognition, voice analysis, and behavioral biometrics, making it more challenging for hackers to steal identities.

For global unique identification, the W3C is setting up a global digital identity network with a decentralized infrastructure. This allows for seamless identification across borders, facilitating international travel, commerce, and communication.

With the evolution of these technologies, digital identity has become seamlessly integrated into everyday life, giving people the confidence to access services on the Internet.

And as new technologies emerge, they will be used to create even more secure, efficient, and user-friendly digital identities. This will help to create a more secure and trustworthy digital world for everyone. As shown in Figure 1-1, the evolution of digital identities has been influenced by technology innovations, social needs, and security and privacy concerns.

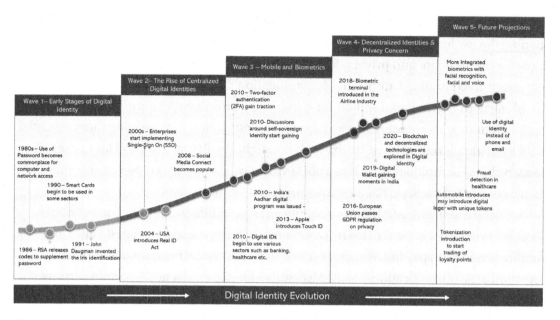

Figure 1-1. *Evolution of digital identities*

Today, in the wake of significant data breaches, especially after the COVID-19 pandemic, we can agree that we need stringent data protection regulations and a decentralized identity framework that emphasizes user control and data privacy.

The Importance of Digital Identities

The importance of digital identities in our interconnected world cannot be overstated because they are crucial as a way to verify identity for security, whether it is accessing a bank account, online services, emails etc. A robust digital identity ensures that only the authorized user can access specific digital resources. With the use of digital identities, organizations can present personalized offers, recommendations, online reviews, etc.

As concerns about data privacy have grown, governments have started creating data privacy laws. This helps users have more control over their personal data, allowing them to decide whom they share their data with and for what purpose.

Many industries also have regulations that require businesses to know their customers and their digital behavior. Digital identities help companies to comply with these regulations by tracking and verifying user activity, and in financial transactions, digital identities help to identify money laundering transactions, terrorist financial transactions, etc.

Overall, digital identities are a cornerstone of the modern digital ecosystem. They not only facilitate secure, efficient, and personalized online transactions but also ensure trust and privacy in an era where these values are paramount. As digital interactions occur globally, digital identities help to safeguard and enhance these interactions.

How Digital Identities Impact Individuals

In a world defined by online interactions, let's consider an example. Nikki's life is inextricably tied to her digital identity. This isn't just the social media profiles she updates or the photos she shares; it encompasses a broader spectrum of digital footprints she leaves behind every time she connects to the virtual world.

From the moment Nikki started her first email account, her digital identity began taking shape. As she grew older, she opened social media accounts on Meta, Instagram, and Twitter; made online purchases on Amazon and Flipkart; and interacted with businesses like her bank, insurance company, and employer that necessitate verifying her identity. Each interaction enriches her digital profile, building an image of Nikki's identity in the online sphere.

With a strong digital identity, Nikki enjoys personalization products based on past purchases, curated playlists in Spotify, and personalized healthcare and connected patient information across hospitals. With the digital identity, the organizations or banking systems analyze the behavior, which makes it easy for an organization to provide more personalized service.

On the downside, Nikki's digital identity has privacy concerns and is exposed to possible identity theft if her credentials are not strong enough. In addition, her social media posts, some written in the heat of teenage emotion, remain accessible years later to anyone following her. For this, the new age SSI/distributed digital identity helps her increase privacy and guard against identity theft.

How Digital Identities Impact Organizations

Digital identities profoundly impact organizations by reshaping operational dynamics, customer relationships, and security protocols. In the age of digital transformation, a clear understanding and management of digital identities enable organizations to deliver personalized customer experiences, leading to enhanced loyalty and increased sales. Moreover, utilizing digital identities ensures tighter security controls, facilitating controlled access to sensitive data and resources and thus reducing the risk of breaches. This security aspect is crucial for compliance with industry-specific regulations, which mandate stringent customer and transactional data protection. However, while digital identities empower businesses with deeper insights into customer behavior and streamline internal processes, they also pose challenges regarding data privacy and integration with the existing systems. As such, organizations must approach digital identity with a blend of strategic enthusiasm and caution, always prioritizing the safety and trust of their customers.

The Value of Trust and Reputation in the Digital Realm

Trust and reputation are pivotal pillars in the expansive digital landscape, directly influencing users' decisions and behaviors. Amid the vastness of online interactions, where face-to-face nuances are absent, users heavily lean on trust to gauge the credibility of platforms and businesses. A sterling reputation can differentiate an entity in a saturated market, foster brand loyalty, and open doors to fruitful collaborations. Conversely, a breach in trust can spell significant setbacks as users seek reliability in their transactions, data security, and information consumption. In essence, trust and reputation aren't just digital assets; they are vital currencies that delineate success from obscurity.

As I mentioned, building trust and reputation in the digital realm requires a commitment to core objectives and values that prioritize the following: user interest, transparency, ethical standards, and adoption of data privacy laws. To build the trust of your customers or users, you must promote integrity, transparency, consistency, accountability, and security, etc., by embedding these values in digital operations and interactions. Organizations need to establish a robust foundation of trust and cultivate a reputation that endears them to the users.

Types of Digital Identities

A digital identity is the data that uniquely identifies a person, device, system, or entity in the digital realm. There are several types of digital identities depending on the subject and the context, as shown in Figure 1-2.

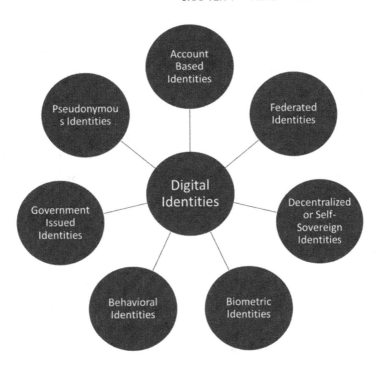

Figure 1-2. *Types of digital identities*

Account-Based Identities

Account-based identities are a form of digital identity associated with online platforms or services. These digital identities are usually linked to usernames, passwords, and personal details.

When you create an account with an online platform such as social media, banking platforms, e-commerce platforms, etc., you create an account-based identity. The account-based identities typically involve personal demographic data and other sensitive information (although some sensitive information might be optional for certain platforms depending on the privacy laws of each country). Behind the scenes, these details are linked to the user ID and password that you create. Some online platforms are secured with various security measures using MFA and secured passwords.

Once you establish an account successfully, you can access the platforms using your credentials, such as the user ID and password. This identity, in the form of an account, represents you when you interact with the services. With this identity, the platform recognizes you and retains your preferences, giving you access to various features.

Let's consider the example of your Facebook account. Your credentials are linked to an account-based identity. When you log in to Facebook, the platform recognizes you and allows you to connect with friends and browse your preferences. It also helps Facebook to send related recommendations to you.

The account-based platform is easy to use, and at this point, it is the most preferred way of managing identities, but it has associated risks. Since these identities are linked to your personal and sensitive information, there are privacy concerns if the data is mishandled. This kind of breach is called a *data breach*. A data breach could involve the exposure of your personal and sensitive information.

Federated Identities

Let's return to the example of Nikki, who regularly uses e-commerce platforms such as Amazon, BestBuy, Flipkart, Alibaba, etc., to shop. For each platform, Nikki had to register on their respective platform separately, which meant creating a separate account with a separate user ID, password, and profile.

As the days and years went by, Nikki began to feel overwhelmed. She had to remember which email and password was used for each platform, reset any password she forgot, update her profile details on each platform, etc. Not to mention, there were numerous verification emails and two-factor authentication steps she had to go through. It was a logistical nightmare.

Federated identities can solve this pain faced by Nikki and other users; various systems or platforms join together and agree to trust each other's credential verification, thereby providing a seamless experience.

Basically, federated identities allow users to use the same credentials across platforms or online services instead of having to create separate credentials for each platform. They allow users to authenticate once and gain access to multiple linked platforms. With federation, Nikki can use her Google or Facebook account to sign in to other sites that support federation. These platforms trust the identity verification of the major players, allowing users to seamlessly navigate the digital landscape without the burden of managing multiple accounts.

In federation, there are multiple parties involved in the process, known as the *identity provider* (IdP) and the *service provider* (SP).

The IdP is a provider that maintains and manages the identity information of users while providing authentication services to relying party applications. The IdP plays a significant role in the federation identities as it plays the role of authenticator and authenticates the credentials on behalf of the platform on which the user is trying to log in. For example, if you are using Google as IdP and you use your Gmail as an authentication mechanism to log in to your platform, then Gmail acts as an IdP. The SP trusts the IdP to validate the user's identity. Once the IdP has confirmed the user's identity, the SP allows users to access its services. Here the SP can be any platform, like your e-commerce platform, streaming platform, etc.; the SP relies on the IdP to authenticate users.

Decentralized Identities and Self-Sovereign Identities

A *decentralized identity* (DID) is a new type of identity that enables verifiable, self-sovereign identities (SSIs). Unlike traditional centralized identifiers like federated identities or account-based identifiers, the DIDs are created, owned, and controlled by the DIDs.

The DID/SSI is a type of identity management that allows you to control your digital identity without depending on a specific identity provider.

The DID/SSI prioritizes user control and autonomy over personal data, unlike the traditional centralized identity verification, where third parties manage and store personal data. The DID/SSI gives individuals full control over their own data. Individuals can store personal data in a secure digital wallet and control who has access to it. By using a DID or SSI, you can prove who you are on e-commerce, online banking, or other services platforms without relying on third-party providers.

The following are the key features of DIDs and SSIs:

- Users are the primary authority for their data.

- DIDs/SSIs operate on a decentralized platform by leveraging blockchain technology to validate and store identities.

- They can be used across different services, platforms, and jurisdictions.

- They use cryptographic methods to secure identities.

- They use open protocols and use a consent mechanism before sharing the details.

- They are designed to exist indefinitely and share only what is required.

- They are platform independent.

As shown in Figure 1-3, in the first step, users create a DID, which is done by generating a public key and a private key. The public key is used to identify the user, and the private key is used to sign and verify DID documents.

In the second step, the user creates a DID document. This document contains a user's DID details, such as a URL, public key, and metadata. The metadata consists of the user's demographic information and other identifying information.

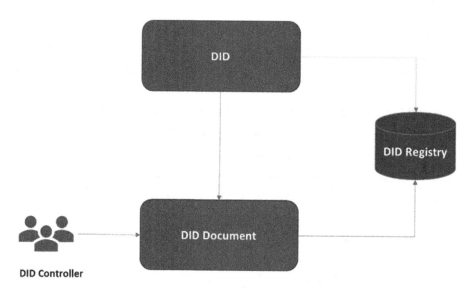

Figure 1-3. *Decentralized identifier*

In the third step, the user publishes the DID document to the DID registry, which is a public database that stores DID documents.

Next, when users interact with any services or platforms like e-commerce, streaming platforms, or social media, they present their DID to the services. These services or platforms use the DID to verify the user's identity and to access the user's metadata.

The DID/SSI is in the early stages of development, but it can potentially revolutionize how we manage identities.

Biometric Identities

Biometric identities use biometric data to recognize and verify individuals based on unique physical and behavioral characteristics such as fingerprint, iris scan, facial recognition, voice recognition, hand geometry, DNA, gait recognition, and keystroke dynamics. This data is stored in a secure data store and can be used to access government services, financial systems, and other sensitive information.

Biometric identification has become increasingly popular because it offers a number of advantages over classic identification such as passwords. For example, biometric data is more difficult to forge than traditional identification and often more convenient for users.

One of the biggest digital identity systems is the Aadhar service in India. Aadhar offers a 12-digit identification number issued by the Unique Identification Authority of India (UIDAI). The Aadhar number uses fingerprints and iris scans to authenticate individuals. Aadhar is used for various purposes in India, including opening a bank account, getting telecom services, and accessing various government services and benefits.

The following are other important examples where biometrics are necessary and more useful than other means of verification:

- Many governments use biometrics identity systems to issue national ID cards and passports.

- Healthcare providers use biometrics identity systems to track patients' records and prevent unauthorized access.

- Financial institutions use biometric identity systems to authenticate customers and prevent fraud.

Biometrics is a promising technology with the potential to improve security, convenience, and customer experience; however, some challenges need to be addressed before it can be widely adopted. These challenges include the following:

- Some individuals are concerned about the privacy implications of biometric data.

- Biometric identity systems can be expensive to implement and to maintain.

- There is a lack of standardization for digital identity systems.

Behavioral Identities

Behavioral identities use biometrics to identify, authenticate, or verify users based on their unique behavioral analytics patterns. This identity approach is based on the idea that each individual has a distinct way of interacting with systems, devices, and platforms.

This identity works by tracking the individual's behavior and identifying patterns over time. For example, this pattern analyzes the the time of day the user logs in, the device the user uses regularly, the applications the user accesses, etc. If a user's behavior deviates from the regular pattern, then this identity can flag the account as suspicious and require additional authentication.

Behavioral identities can be used to protect against various security threats, including password spraying, credential stuffing, account takeover, etc.

Some of the benefits of behavioral identities are improved security and reduced fraud, improved efficiency and user experience, and reduced false positives.

Some of the concerns of behavioral identities are privacy, behavioral changes, and complexities; however, some concerns are mitigated by adopting privacy laws.

Government-Issued Identities

Governments worldwide have started to embrace the potential of digital technology to provide their citizens with secure and easily accessible forms of identification. A government-issued identity is a digital representation of an individual legal identity. This identity consists of the demographic details of an individual of the respective country. These identities are used to verify an individual's identity for various purposes, such as accessing government services, online banking, issuing passports, etc.

Using government-issued identities can offer a range of benefits, such as the following:

- They help to improve security and prevent fraud by requiring individuals to authenticate with a digital identity. Service providers can use these identities to trust an individual.

- It is easier to access services. This can reduce trips to a provider's physical offices.

- There is easy authentication across services as citizens can use a digital identity through their smartphones or other devices.

- Data integrity ensures that the data is updated in real time and is consistent across platforms.

Governments have numerous challenges when implementing digital identities for all citizens, especially in thickly populated and poor economic countries and data privacy as these identities contain an individual's sensitive information.

A few countries have successfully implemented digital identities, and the best example is Aadhar in India. As per UIDAI, India has successfully implemented Aadhar with a 99.9% coverage rate, which equals almost 1.29 billion people as of May 2023. Every enrolled citizen uses Aadhar for all government services, banking systems, insurance, and other services.

Pseudonymous Identities

Pseudonymous identities are the concept of interacting or operating under a pseudonym rather than a real name in digital environments. These identities are used to protect privacy or to create a separate persona.

Let's consider an example where a pseudonymous identity is useful. In the densely populated city of Mumbai, a crime news reporter writes articles and blogs for the *English Daily* and usually uses a pseudonymous identity of the "Silver Line" instead of his real identity. In fact, no one really knows who Silver Line is to this day. Is it a journalist from the *English Daily* or someone from the underworld? Or perhaps an AI tool has gone sentient? The true identity remains shrouded in mystery, but the Silver Line stories are always the talk of the city.

There are many benefits of using pseudonymous identities, and these identities can help to protect privacy and make them less likely to be tracked or identified by others. Pseudonymous identities can empower, protect, and sometimes surprise, offering individuals the freedom to express and act without the constraints tied to their real identity.

However, there are also some risks associated with using pseudonymous identities, as follows:

- It can be difficult to maintain pseudonymous identities.

- If you are using multiple pseudonymous, then it can be difficult to maintain them consistently.

- The pseudonym can be used for malicious purposes. For example, people can use pseudonymous identities to spread misinformation or to commit fraud.

Pseudonymous identities are useful for protecting privacy and creating a separate online persona.

Data Protection and Privacy Standards

Data protection is a central concern in the modern-day digital age. Data protection and privacy standards are a set of rules and regulations that govern how personal data is collected, used, and shared. These standards are used to protect individuals' privacy to ensure that their personal data is not misused. Various standards and regulations have been instituted globally by governments and international organizations. The following are a few of them:

- The European Union's General Data Protection Regulation (GDPR) stands as a comprehensive benchmark, emphasizing user consent, data portability, and breach notifications with 16 exceptions.

- The California Consumer Privacy Act (CCPA) empowers California residents to have control over their personal data.

- Singapore's Personal Data Protection Act (PDPA) empowers Singapore residents to have control over their privacy and personal data.

- The UK's Data Protection Act (DPA) emphasizes transparent data collection, users' rights to their personal data, and stringent consequences for breaches.

- India's Digital Personal Data Protection Law (DPDP) empowers individuals to protect their personal data and provide consent in one of the 22 languages based on user preferences.

- The United States of America's Health Insurance Portability and Accountability Act (HIPAA) provides data privacy and security provisions for safeguarding medical information.

- The U.S. Privacy Act of 1974 is a federal law that establishes a code of fair information practices governing the collection, maintenance, use, and dissemination of personal information about individuals that is maintained in a system of records by federal agencies.

Summary

This chapter provided a comprehensive look at the evolution of digital identities in the context of modern technological, societal, and regulatory changes. It started with a definition of digital identity, breaking down its components and significance. The chapter then delved into how these identities are being redefined by new technologies and paradigms, emphasizing the increasing importance of digital identities in personal and professional spheres. This chapter also provided the profound impacts of digital identities on individuals, including privacy and security considerations, and on organizations, stressing the need for robust identity management systems. The chapter further explored the crucial role of trust and reputation in online interactions and transactions, highlighting different types of digital identities and the technologies enabling them. Overall, the chapter provided good insight into the digital landscape where identity is fluid and multifaceted, underscoring the need for an adaptive, secure, and user-centric identity solution.

CHAPTER 2

Digital Identity Strategy

In today's interconnected digital world, the delineation between our real and virtual selves is fading. As individuals, businesses, and machines transact and communicate more frequently online, the task of managing our digital identities has never been more paramount.

This chapter delves into the essence of a digital identity strategy, highlighting its significance in ensuring security, trust, and privacy in a world that's becoming intrinsically more digital. We'll cover the methodology to assess and implement an effective strategy.

Why You Need a Vision and a Strategy

Digital identity as a concept is becoming increasingly important for enterprises of all sizes. It can help them to improve security, efficiency, and the customer experience. It has emerged as a cornerstone in the evolving digital ecosystem and encapsulates the need for secure, verifiable, and efficient identification for every identity in the digital realm.

The digital realm, with its fluid dynamics and relentless pace, make digital identity an ever-evolving puzzle. Yet, what stands clear among visionary leaders is the understanding that the effort invested in digital identities today will serve as the foundational pillars for the groundbreaking businesses of the future. It's not just a subject of importance to information technology (IT) or cybersecurity; it's a boardroom issue. From chief executive officers (CEOs) to chief financial officers (CFOs) and from chief marketing officers (CMOs) to chief operating officers (COOs), the entire C-suite must recognize the paramount significance of digital identities. In an era where data is the new currency, ensuring its authenticity, security, and appropriate utilization isn't just about avoiding pitfalls. It's about carving out a niche of innovation, trust, and unparalleled value in the marketplace.

© Shivakumar R. Goniwada 2024
S. R. Goniwada, *Introduction to One Digital Identity*, https://doi.org/10.1007/979-8-8688-0255-3_2

The efforts to reimagine digital identities are not just for people but for all things. Just imagine what the next decade of your organization could look like. Does it include the Internet of Things (IoT), where more and more objects are connected to the Internet; the metaverse, where people traverse a persistent digital environment for work or socialization; and the interaction of science and technology, where possibilities like the personalization of medicines can be realized? Digital identity will become the keystone in ensuring that these interactions are personalized, secure, and meaningful. It will determine how we navigate augmented cityscapes, how we interact with sentient AI, and even how our smart homes respond to our preferences.

The C-suite needs to work together to develop a comprehensive digital identity strategy that meets the needs of their business. This strategy should include the following:

- A clear understanding of the risks and challenges of digital identities

- A plan to mitigate these risks and challenges

- A commitment to investing in the right technologies and solutions

- A culture of security and privacy awareness throughout the organization

By taking these steps, the organization can help their businesses and employees to thrive in the digital age.

A strong digital identity strategy can help businesses do the following:

- Protect their customers' data from unauthorized access

- Comply with regulations such as the U.S. Privacy Act of 1974, HIPAA in the United States, GDPR in Europe, DPDP in India, etc.

- Reduce fraud and identity theft and improve the customer experience

- Enable new business models, such as those that rely on blockchain technology or decentralized identity

These are just a few things that the C-suite, policymakers, and society at large will need to grapple with. A strong digital identity strategy is essential for businesses that want to be successful in the digital age.

Strategizing Digital Identities

CIOs must envision a transformative digital landscape where the dispersion of personal identity data across myriad platforms is a relic of the past. Instead, the future relies on the pillars of trust, empowerment, and user-centric control. By centralizing the authority over one's data, users decide its accessibility, viewership, and retention period. In essence, the digital realm will transition from unchecked data dissemination to a structured environment where privacy is not a luxury but a fundamental right. This new blueprint not only fosters confidence among individuals and institutions but also paves the way for a safer, more accountable digital age.

The role of CIO needs to evolve beyond mere IT management, especially in the realm of digital identities. For a CIO, crafting a comprehensive digital identity strategy entails aligning technology, security, and business objectives. This strategy should prioritize creating a unified identity framework that safeguards data integrity and user privacy, while also enabling a seamless user experience across platforms. Integrating advanced authentication mechanisms, such as biometrics or multifactor authentication, is essential to fortify security. Furthermore, CIOs should promote interoperability by adopting open standards, ensuring that identity solutions are adaptable to emerging technologies. Regular audits, in partnership with cybersecurity teams, will ensure compliance with evolving data protection regulations. By actively collaborating with other C-suite members, CIOs ensure that the digital identity strategy not only aligns with current business goals but also anticipates future digital transformation endeavors. In essence, a CIO-led digital identity strategy is a holistic approach that synergizes security, the user experience, and business agility.

To create a successful digital identity strategy, CIOs must ensure the following pieces are part of their strategy:

- The strategy must include the risk and challenges of digital identities, such as data breaches, identity theft, privacy concerns, inaccurate data, fragmented identity solutions, complex user experiences, regulatory challenges, over-reliance on a single point of verification, and most importantly a centralized versus decentralized authority. This can be done by conducting a risk assessment of the organization's digital identity system and process.

- Collaborate with various stakeholders within an organization and also other organizations to understand their perspective and requirements.

- The digital identity implementation is not a big-bang approach; it should be continuously improved upon as technology changes.

- Select the right technology platform to implement the digital identity.

- Educate employees and third parties about changes in the digital identity strategy.

Understanding Today's World Wide Web

The Web was never built with an identity layer, and organizations have increasingly relied on digital technology to run their business. The original design of the Web was for information sharing, and as such, the foundational protocols didn't emphasize user identity and access management. As the Web has evolved into a global platform for various service platforms such as commerce, communication, social media, entertainment, and more, the lack of a native identity mechanism has presented several challenges, such as the following:

- Without a standardized layer, every website and application has had to develop its own authentication layer. This has resulted in a plethora of usernames and passwords, which leads to password fatigue among users.

- The absence of a standard security framework means that many sites implement their own security protocols, some of which might be subpar or outdated. This type of inconsistency results in a range of attacks including phishing, man-in-the-middle attacks, and more.

- Without a standard layer, the user data is scattered across multiple platforms and services. This decentralization makes users try to control their personal information, exacerbating privacy concerns.

- Users often need to create a new account for each digital service, resulting in a fragmented and cumbersome user experience. One way to mitigate this is to use a federation approach, for example, logging in with Google or Facebook.

- Different platforms across the organization or within an organization making interoperability a significant challenge.

- As the Web grew without a built-in identity layer, various regions and countries started introducing regulations regarding digital identity.

Efforts to address these challenges come in the form of identity solutions such as OAuth, OpenID, and single sign-on (SSO). OpenID is an open and decentralized authentication protocol that allows users to log in to multiple websites using a single set of credentials, eliminating the need for multiple usernames and passwords. This is achieved through SSO functionality, improving the user experience by providing a convenient and secure way to access various online services. Still, these are essential patches on the existing system and not a fundamental identity layer of the Web.

As the digital landscape continues to evolve, concepts such as decentralization and self-sovereign identity are gaining momentum. As part of an organization's strategy, the CIO team needs to move to a unified, user-centric, user-friendly, secure identity mechanism.

Using a Digital Identity Strategy in Technology Disruption

The next age of digital technology disruption is being shaped by how our digital and physical worlds intersect. This is being driven by the rise of new technologies such as artificial intelligence (AI), blockchain, IoT, augmented reality/virtual reality (AR/VR), wearable technology, healthcare evolution, autonomous vehicles, and much more. These technologies are making it possible to create a more seamless and secure connection between our digital and physical identities. Digital identity is at the epicenter of this exchange and is essential if CIOs are to thrive in this new era.

Here's how the technology disruption amplifies the role of digital identity as a foundation pillar:

- With the evolution of IPv6, every device will be digitally connected to the Internet, each with its unique identity. So, there's a growing need for a robust digital identities framework that can ensure communication, data exchange, and operation.

- As VR/AR technologies become more immersive and integrated into daily life, digital avatars and identities in the metaverse will play a pivotal role. These identities will govern our interactions, purchases, and access within virtual worlds and digital overlays on the physical world.

21

- Urban centers are evolving around the world with interconnected hubs of technologies. From traffic management to utilities, the seamless operation of smart cities hinges on the effective management of digital identities for devices, services, and citizens.

- Devices worn on the body, from fitness to health, are continuously collecting data and interfacing with other systems for analysis. These interactions need reliable digital identities.

- Cloud identity management (CIM) is a set of technologies and services used to manage identities and access controls in a cloud environment. CIM enables organizations to securely authenticate users, manage user identities, and control access to resources and services across various cloud-based and on-premises applications. CIM provides various capabilities such as SSO, MFA, directory services, user provisioning features, and access management.

To support technology disruptions, several digital identity frameworks are to be used to ensure the creation, management, and utilization of digital identities. These frameworks provide a structural approach for handling complex identity challenges in an evolving digital landscape. Some of the popular frameworks are OpenID, federated identity management, self-sovereign identities (SSIs), and decentralized identifiers (DIDs).

Let's consider an example of the healthcare management platform b.well, which is working to improve healthcare experiences by providing a unified platform that allows patients to access their health information and services digitally.[1] This data exists across various platforms not only in b.well but in hospitals, insurance companies, etc. This complexity makes b.well force users to authenticate in every platform. This can mean not only digitally but also physically by showing physical IDs.

b.well saw these challenges and its unhappy customers and partnered with Mastercard to build a new intelligent identity platform. The platform uses Mastercard's ID verification service to provide a more secure and convenient way for patients to prove their identity when accessing healthcare services. This identity platform uses

---

[1] https://www.icanbwell.com/

a combination of government ID document scanning, facial biometrics with liveness detection, and mobile phone intelligence to verify the identity of the patients. This makes the platform more secure and difficult for hackers to gain access to.

To access this platform, patients need to provide a scanned government ID and a selfie taken with a mobile phone. With this information, the platform can verify the authenticity of the patient and give them access.

With this disruption, b.well was able to increase security, improve the user experience, and provide added convenience for its patients. The entire experience offers a glimpse into the future trajectory of digital identities. The future of digital identities uses biometrics, decentralization, AI, and blockchain to store data. Every CIO needs to recognize that digital identity as a concept isn't a technology question; it's strategic business imperative.

As another example, the Electronic Personal Identification Consortium (EPIC) is a platform that uses DIDs to give individuals control over their personal data. Individuals are not reliant on any single company or government for their identity management; instead, individuals can create and control their own unique identifiers. This method greatly enhances data security and privacy, making personal information much more challenging to compromise. Individuals have granular control over who accesses their data and how it is used, empowering them with unprecedented personal data sovereignty. Additionally, EPIC facilitates smother access to a wide array of services, both online and offline, by simplifying the verification process and reducing the risks of identity theft and fraud. This process involves creating a DID, securely storing it, and then using it across various service platforms. This platform is still under development and might provide even more promising solutions to the DID ecosystem.

Introducing the Digital Identity Strategy Maturity Framework

The Digital Identity Strategy Maturity Framework serves as a roadmap, enabling organizations to understand their current capabilities, identify gaps, and plot a path forward. As shown in Figure 2-1, the y-axis shows the user access level, and the x-axis shows the security, governance, and compliance.

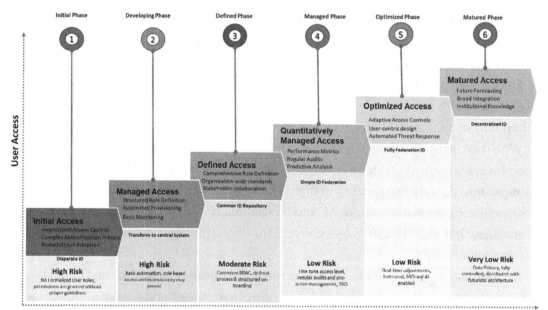

Figure 2-1. *The Digital Identity Strategy Maturity Framework*

Beginning from the bottom left and moving to the bottom right along the x-axis, you can see the level of risk associated with all six phases, determined by the types of tools and processes an organization currently uses. For example, an organization that does not have a digital identity strategy and no formalized user rules or proper guidelines results in high risk. This high risk indicates the organization should immediately consider solutions that will move them toward the right on the x-axis.

Beginning at the bottom left to the top left along the y-axis, you can see the user access levels associated with the six phases. Being at the top means the organization has optimized its access management for secure user access by adhering to privacy regulations.[2]

This Digital Identity Strategy Maturity Framework serves as a strategic roadmap for organizations looking to fortify their digital identity initiatives and prioritize their technological investments based on the present status. The framework delineates six progressive phases of identity maturity, each characterized by an escalating level of compliance, security, and user accessibility. As organizations transition from one phase to another, they not only refine the current identity processes but also integrate

---

[2] https://www.imprivata.com/digital-identity-maturity-models

advanced digital identity tools that adhere to the organization's security, compliance, and other regulations. By following this approach, the organization can pinpoint the current position, recognize the tangible steps needed for advancement, and ensure a comprehensive and unified approach to its digital identity program. In essence, this framework offers both a diagnostic lens to evaluate existing structures and a prescriptive pathway to achieve greater digital identity futuristic sophistication.

Initial Phase

This phase is prior to implementing a formal digital strategy. In this phase there is no central repository for user identities and permissions, and user management is done manually and siloed across different departments. The lack of a unified systems amplifies the overall risk profile. Without a systematic and well-governed approach, the organization's digital identity infrastructure remains vulnerable, leaving both assets and data exposed to potential threats.

Developing Phase

In the developing phase, the organization is strategically leveraging cutting-edge tools to fortify its security posture. With well-structured and manageable IT processes already in operation and a focused approach on safeguarding critical applications, the groundwork for a robust digital identity framework has been laid. This initial emphasis on tools signifies a proactive stance toward security, aiming to establish a resilient foundation for more advanced identity and access management (IAM) practices. The implementation of these measures demonstrates a commitment not only to protect sensitive information but also to streamline access management in a controlled and efficient manner.

Evolving Phase

In this phase, the organization has reached a well-defined level of maturity and painstakingly crafted comprehensive role definitions that clearly delineate access privileges and responsibilities for various user groups. These role definitions ensure that access permissions align closely with job functions and mitigate the risk of unauthorized access and potential security breaches.

Furthermore, in this phase, the organization has successfully established organization-wide standards governing IAM policies, procedures, and technical controls. The IAM uses the individuals in a system, controlling their access to resources within that system by associating user rights and restrictions and providing administrators with the tools and technologies to change roles, audit user activities, and publish reports. These standardized practices provide a cohesive framework for managing digital identities consistently across entire enterprises, enhancing efficiency and security. Collaboration among stakeholders, including IT, security teams, business units, and compliance functions, has become a hallmark of this phase. This collaboration ensures that IAM practices are aligned with broader organizational objectives and that everyone is on the same page regarding identity and access management strategies. There are various IAM tools available, such as Microsoft IAM, SailPoint, IBM Tivoli, etc.

In this phase, there is an improvement in compliance and a centralized view of compliance requirements that spans ecosystems. This comprehensive plan allows for a strategic and efficient approach to meeting regulatory and industry-specific mandates, which further bolsters an organization's security posture.

Managed Phase

In this phase, the organization has made a significant advancement with the introduction of performance metrics to quantitatively assess the effectiveness. These metrics provide valuable insight into the efficiency of access controls, user provisioning, and overall security postures. By monitoring these metrics, organizations can make informed decisions to further enhance IAM. In this phase, organizations maintain a secure environment with regular audits for ensuring that digital identity policies and procedures are being followed consistently.

This phase will introduce predictive analytics to help organizations anticipate potential security risks and proactively implement measures to mitigate them.

Optimized Phase

In the optimized phase of the Digital Identity Strategy Maturity Framework, organizations have achieved a high level of sophistication and maturity in the approach to digital identities. Organizations have implemented adaptive access control, a dynamic approach that assesses various contextual factors in real time to determine appropriate access levels. This ensures that access privileges are continuously aligned with a user's roles, locations, and activities, enhancing security and usability.

Furthermore, organizations in this phase prioritize user-centric design in digital identity strategies. This means that user experience and convenience are central considerations in the design and implementation of access management processes. By placing the user at the forefront, organizations can strike a balance between security and user-friendly interactions, resulting in a more seamless and efficient user experience.

The automated threat response is another important step in this phase. Organizations have integrated advanced technologies and intelligent systems to detect and respond to security threats in real time. This proactive approach significantly reduces the response time to potential breaches, fortifying the organization's overall security approach.

Along with the best-of-breed security governance and approaches, the organization is working toward solving any privacy and regulatory concerns.

Matured Phase

Currently, the matured phase is the ultimate phase of the digital identity. If the organization has reached this level, then it is checking all the boxes of the digital identity. This phase is characterized by a combination of advanced features that set the organization apart in terms of security, efficiency, privacy, and adaptability.

In this phase, the organization possesses a capability for future forecasting, which has harnessed cutting-edge technologies and advanced analytical tools to not only respond to current challenges but also anticipate future threats and business challenges. This forward-thinking approach enables the organization to proactively adjust digital identity strategies to stay ahead of the curve.

Digital identities are seamlessly woven into the fabric of the entire ecosystem including for internal and external, partners and the cloud. This comprehensive integration ensures a unified approach to digital identity and seamless experiences while maintaining robust security controls.

Reaching this phrase means having a wealth of institutional knowledge combined with steadfast commitment to data privacy. Organizations have accumulated a deep understanding of digital identity best practices through years of experience. Additionally, the organization has established a culture of privacy protection, ensuring that sensitive data is handled with the utmost care and compliance with relevant regulations being paramount.

Using the Framework to Assess an Organization

Assessing where an organization stands with regard to digital identities by using the Digital Identity Strategy Maturity Framework involves a structured approach to evaluating various aspects of the organization's capabilities against conformance, as shown in Figure 2-2.

Feature/Conformance	Ad-Hoc	Basic	Consistent	Complaint	Conformance	Fully Complaint
Governance & Administration	○					
Access Control	◖					
Identity Management	◖					
Prediction & Analytics	○					
Auditing & Compliance	○					
Broad Integration	○					
Automation	○					
Stakeholder Collaboration	○					
Privacy	○					
Strategic Alignment	○					

Ad-Hoc – Initial Phase, Basic – Developing Phase, Consistent – Evolving Phase, Complaint – Managed Phase, Conformance – Optimized Phase, Fully Complaint – Matured Phase

○ Not Managed ◖ Available but only system/application specific ◗ Available and consistently done across departments ◖ Available and consistently done across enterprises ● Fully Available

Figure 2-2. *Capabilities and conformance*

The steps involved in conducting an assessment of a digital strategy are as follows:

1. Understand the framework and features/capabilities of digital identity.

2. Collect various information across enterprises by discussing it with the CIO, CTO, and security, application, and integration teams.

3. Establish the assessment conformance/criteria, as shown in Figure 2-2.

4. Assess the business and technical strategy for alignment with goals, adaptability, customer-centricity, and privacy.

5. Evaluate the digital identity infrastructure with the technology stack, scalability and interoperability, and security measures.

6. Review security methods such as identity management and access control.

7. Review access compliance such as regulatory and privacy.

Once you have data, rate the maturity of all the features with Harvey balls, as shown in Figure 2-2. This provides a clear indication of the organization's current state.

By following these detailed steps, you can effectively assess and map your organization using the Digital Identity Strategy Maturity Framework. This digital identity maturity framework provides invaluable insights for improvement and strategic growth.

Developing a Digital Identity Strategy

Developing a digital identity strategy is a multifaceted approach. At its core, this strategy outlines a structured way to manage and secure digital identities, encompassing a wide array of components and considerations. Before the development, you need to use the maturity framework as depicted in this chapter to assess the current state of the digital identity.

The development requires a thorough understanding of the current technological landscape, including the existing digital identity systems, security protocols, and compliance standards. In addition, stakeholders from various departments such as IT, security, compliance, legal, etc., must be engaged to ensure a holistic approach.

The development of a digital identity strategy has the potential to revolutionize the way the users interact with a platform. Users must be comfortable with accessing online services, making purchases, and participating in civic life online. So, the development of digital identity strategy encompasses the design and implementation as it is a rapidly evolving field, and there are numerous new technologies that are being developed to improve the security and convenience of digital identities. These technologies include blockchain, quantum cryptography, federal learning, etc.

However, numerous challenges need to be addressed before digital identities are widely adopted. These challenges are security, privacy, interoperability, and acceptance.

Creating a Digital Identity Strategy Roadmap

A digital identity roadmap involves a structured plan to guide the design, implementation, and operation of digital identities within an ecosystem and extended ecosystem for the internal and external users.

For the roadmap, you need to follow these steps:

1. Conduct a maturity assessment.

2. Define the scope and convert it to an integrated backlog.

3. Identity the stakeholders.

4. Evaluate the design and technology.

5. Map the user experience and journey.

6. Implement a pilot.

7. Monitor the pilot with real cases with few internal and external users.

8. Industrialize the digital identity.

9. Monitor and optimize.

10. Implement compliance and security measures.

Evaluating the Digital Identity Strategy

Evaluating a digital identity strategy involves a thorough assessment of its effectiveness and impact on identity management in an enterprise. The evaluation is essential to ensure that the strategy aligns with its intended goals and delivers the anticipated benefits.

Let's consider Organization A. This organization is implementing a biometric authentication system as part of its digital identity strategy. Organization A's primary objective is to enhance security and streamline the user authentication process by keeping privacy in mind. To evaluate the strategy, Organization A establishes key performance indicators (KPIs) and metrics. These indicators include the adoption rate of biometric factors, which indicates how many customers are enrolled in and actively using the new authentication method. User feedback is another critical aspect; this can be measured through usability testing, and the institution assesses how easily customer can enroll their biometrics. User surveys and feedback loops allow customers to provide insight into their experience.

Security, auditing, and compliance considerations are paramount, so Organization A conducts regular audits that help to identify vulnerabilities in the authentication process, i.e., biometric in this case. An incident response process tests Organization A's readiness to handle security breaches.

Another important criteria is privacy. This metric ensures that customer data is handled in compliance with the data protection regulations of each country. In this case, Organization A needs to ensure that the biometric data is stored securely or processed in a decentralized approach where the customer can control the privacy.

Another important metric is cost-benefit analysis. This metric is essential in understanding the financial implications of the strategy. Organization A compares the cost of implementing the biometric system against the benefits of increased security and improved user experience. This analysis helps determine the return on investment (ROI).

Another important consideration is identity analytics. This analytics focuses on enhancing the IAM system through insights derived from data. The insights involves collecting and analyzing data related to user behavior, access patterns, and security threats to make informed decisions about IAM controls. By applying advanced analytics and machine learning techniques to IAM System to detect and predict security risks, understand user behavior, that ensure compliance and regulatory requirements. Organization A takes a proactive approach to identify anomalies, suspicious activities, or potential breaches by recognizing patterns that deviate from normal behavior.

Furthermore, Organization A continuously monitors compliance with industry standards and regulations such General Data Protection Regulations (GDPR) and the Digital Personal Data Protection (DPDP) Act. The organization conducts regular audits within the organization and with third-party auditors.

Lastly, Organization A evaluates the digital identity strategy with scalability and future proofing. This helps Organization A verify that their biometric implementation can accommodate future technologies such as decentralization and self-sovereign identities. This ensures the strategy is going in the right direction without reinventing technologies.

In a nutshell, evaluating a digital identity strategy involves a comprehensive approach that includes measuring KPIs, gathering user feedback, ensuring security and privacy, conducting cost-benefit analysis, monitoring compliance, and planning for future-proofing.

Selecting a Digital Identity Technology

Technology selection is a key phase in a digital identity strategy that involves choosing the appropriate technology, tools, and platforms to implement and manage digital identities. Factors in the technology selection process include the requirements, user experiences, privacy and regulatory requirements, scalability and compatibility, and cost and support.

1. Gather requirements. In this case, you need to conduct an assessment using the maturity framework shown in Figure 2-2. The output of the maturity assessment is the requirement input to the selection process.

2. Evaluate the technology and options. In this step, you need to check on what type of protocols you require, such as OpenID Connect, OAuth, and Security Assertion Markup Language (SAML), and assess the feasibility and effectiveness of incorporating biometric authentication methods such as fingerprint, facial recognition, etc., and distributed identities with blockchain and self-sovereign identity.

3. Verify the scalability and future proofing, and make sure any tool is compatible with the existing identity landscape.

4. Verify the security technology such as the encryption mechanism and ensure the technology is aligned with the compliance and regulatory requirements.

5. Verify the technology against the user experience and make sure it works cross-platform; in addition, keep an eye on emerging technologies.

6. The final step is to check the costs. You can verify the total cost of ownership (TCO) to evaluate the licensing costs and support costs along with vendor and community support costs.

By considering these steps, you can make informed decisions and select the right technology for your organization that meets the organizational strategy and vision.

Summary

This chapter provided a comprehensive guide for organizations looking to navigate the complex landscape of digital identities in the modern era. It began by setting a clear vision and overarching strategy, emphasizing the role of CIOs and other leaders in steering digital identity initiatives. The chapter acknowledged the challenges and opportunities presented by today's Web and how technology disruptions like AI, blockchain, IoT, quantum computing, etc., are reshaping identity management. This chapter also provided a Digital Identity Strategy Maturity Framework to help organizations assess their current state and identify areas for improvement. Further, it guided you through the development of a robust digital identity strategy, outlining steps to create a detailed and actionable roadmap. Finally, this chapter provided methods for evaluating the effectiveness and efficiency of digital identity strategies, ensuring they align with broader business goals, enhance security, improve user experience, and comply with evolving regulatory frameworks. This chapter is a critical resource for organizations wanting to leverage digital identities as a strategic asset in the digital age.

CHAPTER 3

Foundation of Future Digital Identity

As explained in previous chapters, authentication is one of the most crucial functions in the entire security process. The future of digital identities rests on authentication with biometric factors, as this is the safest way to authenticate critical information. This chapter discusses the foundations of using digital identities in the future to secure your information. These topics are very new, and various organizations and researchers are still working on developing some of them.

The following concepts collectively form any forward-thinking digital identity based on future technologies. Adhering to these concepts will help build trust between organizations and their users, fostering a secure, compliant, and seamless digital environment.

Identity Fluidity

Identity fluidity in the digital realm is the concept of allowing digital identities to be dynamic, adaptable, and contextually flexible. This concept guides organizations away from a static identity model to a dynamic identity model with personalized representation. With identity fluidity, the identity may change or adapt based on various factors such as preferences, context of interaction, etc. This concept recognizes that people may present themselves differently in various online spaces or platforms or may adopt different perspectives in various contexts.

In traditional static digital identity systems like we are all currently using, an individual online identity is often represented by a fixed set of attributes, for example name, email, phone, etc.

© Shivakumar R. Goniwada 2024
S. R. Goniwada, *Introduction to One Digital Identity*, https://doi.org/10.1007/979-8-8688-0255-3_3

The *identity fluidity* concept will help users to do the following:

- Adjust themselves dynamically for different roles

- Choose who they want to be in public and in private

- Provide full privacy for certain contexts

Let's consider an example where identity fluidity is appropriate. Nikki is a software engineer executive. In her professional life, Nikki maintains a polished and authoritative online presence. For example, on LinkedIn, she shares content related to software architecture and engineering, attends webinars, and connects and follows related industry executives. This professional identity showcases her expertise and experience in the software industry.

However, outside of her work life, on weekends or on holidays, Nikki is interested in farming and shares her experience and love of farming. She started selling fruits from her farm, writes blog posts related to farming, and connects with related farming technologies. In this context, she presents different aspects of her identity, focusing on her passion of farming. The content of the blog posts is more informal compared to the professional content posted on LinkedIn.

Additionally, Nikki is an active participant in various charities and social services. In this space, she talks to various leaders, charity organizations, etc. This persona is entirely different from her other two.

In this way, Nikki's digital identity is fluid. She presents different facets of herself in different online environments, adapting to the specific context and audience. This fluidity allows Nikki to express various interests and aspects of her personality without any contradiction or conflict.

There is no direct or standard technology tools to implement identity fluidity because it is not a specific technology; it is a concept that you can include in your existing technology solution by providing the ability to modify different personas.

In your system, you can consider including flexibility in user profiles so users can update and modify personal information easily, supporting multiple identities in a single system, and including security measures to address privacy concerns.

Augmented Reality Digital Identity

Digital identities have evolved beyond mere username and passwords. Now you need to have a digital identity seamlessly merge with augmented reality, creating a new dimension of interactive and immersive experiences. Digital identities have become an integral part of augmented reality existences, intertwining seamlessly with the physical world.

Picture a world where your online self blends effortlessly with the world you see through special glasses or screens. When you put on these special glasses, your digital self appears as a colorful character that moves and reacts. In this case, you don't need to remember passwords anymore. Instead, the glasses integrate with the digital identity to recognize your face and eyes to authenticate. For this, you need to have different digital identities to make the virtual world feel like a natural part of reality.

You can use this concept to change how a digital identity works in AR. Here are some examples:

- The passwords and PINs are replaced with a facial recognition or iris scanner tool. The AR glasses integrate with the digital identity to authenticate users in real time, ensuring a secure and personalized experience.

- Each individual digital identity is represented by a dynamic, customizable avatar. These avatars respond to emotions, body language, and environmental stimuli, creating a lifelike representation of the user in the digital realm.

- Digital identities seamlessly integrate with identity management software to help avatars in meetings and collaborative projects, facilitating a natural extension of their physical presence.

- Integrating with social media is important as platforms are no longer confined to screens. Users engage in immersive social experiences through AR. Shared spaces become dynamic, enabling real-time interactions, shared experiences, and a deeper sense of community.

- Robust encryption and decentralization ensure the users maintain control over their personal information. You can achieve this by using blockchain technology and advanced encryption.

Biometric Artistry

The evolution of biometric authentication extends far beyond traditional classic user ID and password methods. This concept is about using biometric factors with gesture recognition, emotional analysis, and DNA-based authentication for identity verification.

Gesture recognition enables users to authenticate themselves through unique movement or hand signals by adding a dynamic and personalized layer of security. Emotion analysis leverages facial expression and other psychological cues for identity verification and ensures only the rightful user gains access.

An important and secure authentication mechanism is the DNA-based authentication, where an individual's genetic code serves as the identification. This method is very highly secured as each individual possesses a truly one-of-a-kind genetic makeup. This type of authentication is useful for accessing very highly classified and sensitive information.

If you want to implement this concept, you need to have the following capabilities for gesture recognition:

- Utilize specialized hardware components such as depth-sensing cameras or infrared sensors to capture fine-grained gestures.

- Combine data from sensing cameras or sensors to accurately track and interpret hand and body movements.

- Create and train deep learning models to recognize and classify various gestures. Techniques like convolutional neural networks (CNNs) are particularly effective for recognition.

- Implement high-speed data processing algorithms to ensure swift and responsive gesture recognition.

You need to have the following capabilities in emotional analysis:

- Use high-resolution cameras to capture facial expressions. Apply machine learning models such as CNNs and recurrent neural networks (RNNs) for real-time emotions.

- Extract relevant features of facial landmarks, such as the position of eyes, eyebrows, and mouth to infer emotions accurately.

- Build a comprehensive database of facial expressions mapped to the corresponding emotions to enhance accuracy.

You can find this implementation in the cross-border smart gateway used in Dubai International Airports.

You need to have the following capabilities for DNA-based authentication:

- Use a specialized kit to collect a biological sample from individuals.

- Use advanced DNA sequencing techniques such as next-generation sequencing (NGS) or polymerase chain reaction (PCR) for rapid and accurate analysis of genetic details.

- Store encrypted genetic information in a secure, decentralized database by keeping high security and privacy.

- If the sequence matches the reference sequence, then the individual is authenticated.

DNA-based authentications are used in identity verification, forensics, luxury art and goods, and passports. They are highly accurate and reliable but not infallible due to cost, complexity, and privacy.

Emotional Intelligence in Authentication

Emotional intelligence in authentication employs technology to gauge and interpret emotional responses during the authentication process. For instance, in facial recognition, as a user attempts to log in, the authentication system captures the face image of the user and employs advanced algorithms to analyze the facial expression. Usually, these algorithms are trained to recognize the emotions of the face such as joy, stress, etc. If the system detects any uncommon recognition of the user's face, then it prompts the user for additional authentication factors. A similar approach is used for voice recognition, but in the AI age, the voice can be manipulated easily.

By integrating these emotional cues with biometric data, behavioral patterns, and contextual information, the system forms an emotional profile that helps to verify the authenticity of the user. You can see this type of authentication in cross-border immigration centers.

The implementation of emotional intelligence authentication starts with data collection and goes through adaptive responses.

1. The system first captures images or videos of the face and voice by using cameras and microphones and tracks the behavioral patterns of the eyebrows, cheeks, lips, etc., in the case of facial recognition, and voice modulation in the case of voice.

2. Algorithms analyze the facial expression, eyebrow movement, cheeks movement, lips movement, smiles, etc., by using deep learning and natural language processing (NLP). Audio analysis algorithms examine the voice tone, pitch, rhythm, intensity, etc.

3. Once the emotions are detected, the output is to categorize these emotions into multiple states such as happiness, stress, anxiety, or anger; you can do this by using machine learning (ML) models trained on the labeled dataset.

4. The next step is to capture the contextual parameters such as the user's location, time of day, and recent activities, which may influence the emotion categorization.

5. Based on the emotional data, contextual information, and predefined rules and algorithms, the system provides a confidence score for the authentication attempt.

6. Depending on the score, the system decides whether to authenticate, require further analysis, check with the operations team, etc.

Neuro-Authentication or Brainwave Authentication

Neuro-authentication or brainwave authentication leverages the brainwave activity pattern to verify a person's identity. Activity such as an electroencephalogram (EEG) and other neuroimaging techniques are used to capture and analyze the electrical signals generated by neurons in the brain. The data is then analyzed by the neuro-authentication engine to create a unique brainwave signature for the individual.

To authenticate the individual, an individual needs to repeat the same activity of putting on an EEG device and allowing the system to analyze their brain waves. If the brainwaves match the signature that is stored in the system, the individual is authenticated and otherwise declined.

Each individual possesses unique brainwave patterns, akin to a neurological fingerprint. With the specific algorithm and hardware, the neuro-authentication translates these patterns into an actual authentication.

The neuro-authentication architecture includes multiple components, as shown in Figure 3-1. The architecture is a combination of high-powered hardware and software components.

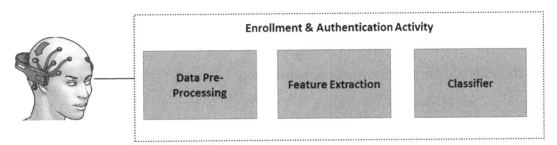

Figure 3-1. *Neuro or brainwave authentication*

The components are as follows:

- **Data acquisition:** Data acquisition consists of an EEG device; it is the primary hardware used to capture brain waves.

- **Feature extraction:** This component converts raw EEG data into meaningful features such as the following:

  - **Signal processing:** This will analyze the EEG data to extract features that can be used to create a unique brainwave signature.

  - **Feature extraction algorithm:** This algorithm extracts the features from EEG data.

- **Classifier:** This is a matching pattern that can differentiate between brainwave pattern of different individuals. This component consists of the following:

  - **Matching rules:** This contains the matching rules that compare the extract data to the enrolled data.

  - **Decision rules:** This decides whether to authenticate the user based on the matching rules.

This type of authentication is highly complicated and will be used when you require authentication in highly sensitive places such as military facilities, medical records, and medical drug transportation.

These are the pros of this authentication mechanism:

- Very secure authentication because it is difficult to spoof brain waves and difficult to hack

- Convenient way of authentication as you don't need to hold password or fingerprint data

These are the cons of this type of authentication:

- The EEG device is expensive.

- The process is slow due to the analysis methods.

Multisensory Authentication

Multisensory authentication is the combination of touch, sight, and sound, or any of the two. This combined paradigm offers a synergistic layering of security measures. By integrating visual recognition with auditory memory and tactile response, you not only amplify security but also make the process more immersive and difficult to spoof. This type of authentication harnesses the strengths of each sensory input, requiring a potential intruder to bypass multiple intertwined layers of security. This process elevates your security to a higher level.

Let's consider a Department of Treasury, which operates and maintains systems that are critical to the financial infrastructure of a country, such as coin and currency production. To enter into these areas, the Department of Treasury installs the MSA procedure. Before entering into this area, the employee might see a multisensory biometric verification procedure such as fingerprint, iris scanner, etc. The combined sensory cues, unique to each login attempt, make it extremely difficult for potential attackers to predict or replicate.

A properly designed MSA can offer enhanced security without compromising on the user experience. The MSA system typically uses a combination of biometrics, behavioral, and contextual sensory modalities. The biometric authentication methods uses the physical and behavioral characteristics to identify an individual, such as fingerprints, facial recognition, voice recognition, or iris scanning. The behavioral authentication uses an individual's unique patterns of behavior to identify them, such as typing pattern, gait analysis, or mouse movement patterns. The contextual method uses information about an individual's environment to identify them such as location, time of day, or device type.

MSA consists of sensors, feature extraction, and a matching and decision module, as shown in Figure 3-2. The sensors capture data from individuals using a fingerprint scanner, a camera, an iris scanner, or a microphone. Once the scanners collect the information, the future extraction tool extracts relevant features from the sensor data. For example, the fingerprint scanner extracts the minutiae points from the fingerprint image. Once the information is collected, the matching algorithm compares the extracted features to an existing individual's information in a database. If the match is found, then the individual will be authenticated (otherwise declined), and the decision module determines whether to authenticate the user based on the result of the matching module. The decision module matches with other sensory details such as the iris along with the fingerprint type. Once all the matching criteria are successful, the individual is authenticated.

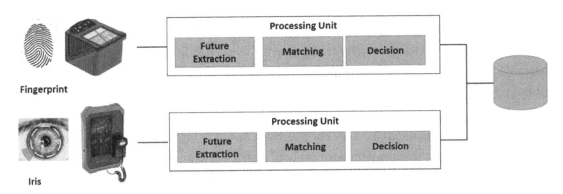

Figure 3-2. MSA process

MSA provides various benefits such as enhanced security, reduced fraud, and improved user experience, but it comes with a few challenges such as cost, complexity, and privacy.

Dynamic Avatar Identities

Dynamic avatar identities are digital representations of individuals in a virtual space like the metaverse, virtual gaming, etc. Static identities remain consistent until you change the identity, but a dynamic avatar offers a fluidity for interaction depending on the context.

Creating a dynamic avatar identity is a multistep process that uses AI, ML models NLP, and other criteria depending on where this avatar will be used.

The first step is to identify the context where this avatar is to be used and then design the avatar's appearance and model, including clothing, appearance, animation, facial features, voice, and body shape. AI-powered tools play a crucial role in shaping the visual and auditory identity of the avatar, ensuring a rich and personalized virtual presence. For the visual aspects, AI allows users to choose from a wide array of clothing styles and adapt their look in real time to suit different contexts within the virtual environment. Facial features can be intricately sculpted using AI, enabling precise adjustments to expressions, hairstyles, and other characteristics to reflect the user's desired appearance or emotional state. Body shape customization is another aspect where AI contributes, allowing for the adjustment of body proportions to represent a diverse range of physical identities accurately. AI's role extends to voice customization; it can generate unique voices that either mimic the user's own speech patterns or create entirely new vocal identities. Additionally, AI can imbue these voices with emotional depth, enabling the avatar to express a wide range of emotions through vocal cues.

The next step is to train the avatar by using ML and NLP. In the process of creating dynamic avatars, training with ML and NLP is important for achieving behavioral modeling and natural language understanding. ML models are trained on a vast array of user interactions to adapt and personalize the avatar's behavior according to individual preferences, styles, etc. They are also adept at interpreting social cues, allowing the avatar to respond appropriately to nuance and changes in the social and conversational context. On the other hand, NLP is fundamental in endowing avatars with conversational abilities, enabling them to engage in natural language dialogues that are coherent, contextual relevant, and nuanced.

The next step is deploying the avatar in a virtual environment. The deployment involves integration and refinement. Once the avatar is designed, personalized, and trained using AI, ML, and NLP technologies, it's ready to be integrated into the intended virtual spaces, such as gaming platforms, social VR, or the metaverse. This integration process ensures that the avatar functions smoothly within the environment's unique technical and social ecosystem, interacting appropriately with other avatars, users, and virtual elements. Following integration, extensive testing is conducted to assess the avatar's performance, responsiveness, and overall user experience. A successful deployment results in a dynamic avatar that is not only visually and conversationally realistic but also fully adapted to the virtual environment, ready to provide users with an engaging virtual presence.

Creating a dynamic avatar is complex, and the following are the basic steps. You need to have a 3D modeling tool to create an avatar.

1. Sketch and create an initial avatar.

2. Create a 3D model by using various tools such as Blender, Autodesk Maya, and so on.

3. Create an interface where the avatar can choose parameters for dynamic features such outfit, real-time emotions, etc.

Quantum-Resistant Encryption or Post-Quantum Cryptography

Quantum-resistant encryption or post-quantum cryptography encompasses cryptographic algorithms specifically designed to withstand the computational capabilities of quantum computers.

Quantum computers are a new type of computer that use the principle of quantum mechanics to perform calculations. Quantum mechanics studies the behavior of matter at the atomic and subatomic level. Quantum computers use superposition and entanglement to perform calculations that are impossible for traditional computers. For example, a quantum computer could factor a large number into its prime factors much faster than traditional computers. This could have implications for cryptography, as many encryption algorithms rely on the difficulty of factoring large numbers. You can read more about it on Google.[1]

The traditional cryptographic methods such as RSA (Rivest-Shamir-Adleman) and ECC (Elliptic Curve Cryptography) are powerful for today's technology but not suitable for the more powerful quantum world that uses the algorithms like Shor's.[2] Quantum-resistance encryption counteracts this vulnerability by using different mathematical structures that become hard for quantum computers.

---

[1] https://quantumai.google/
[2] https://en.wikipedia.org/wiki/Shor%27s_algorithm

AI-Powered Identity Guardians

An AI-powered identity is not an actual authentication mechanism, but it protects user identities from fraud and theft by using AI algorithms. Unlike the present cybersecurity measures, this guardian continuously learns about and acts on any new emerging threats and users' behaviors and provides dynamic defense mechanisms. You can use this type of identity for personal use or for an entire enterprise.

These guardians operate through an AI technique with cybersecurity protocols (access control, authentication, information protection, and automated monitoring). The guardians continuously analyze user data and activities in real time by using ML models. ML models enable the guardians to process and identify patterns from complex datasets, such login behaviors, biometric input, network access points, and phishing attempts. When guardians identify an anomaly or potential threat, they take immediate action such alerting the user, blocking access, etc.

The neural network helps guardians to analyze the user behavior by training on the user's past behaviors, such as login time, device usage pattern, behavior, etc. It is very complex to train as you need to have a combination of all the user's behaviors. To simplify the training process, you need to create a set of related user patterns to train, and deep learning helps guardians process biometric authentication.

NLP helps guardians analyze emails and messages for signs of phishing attempts. NLP is trained to understand the semantics and structure of language to detect malicious intent or suspicious links. Guardians have already been established throughout enterprises to protect against phishing.

Incorporating AI-powered guardians provides a robust and dynamic defense mechanism that can respond to a broad spectrum of threats to digital identities.

Summary

This chapter delved into the evolution and future of digital identities, emphasizing the technological advancements and conceptual shifts that are shaping the digital identity landscape. It began with the concept of identity fluidity, recognizing the increasingly dynamic and multifaceted nature of personal identity in digital spaces. The chapter then explored the integration of augmented reality in digital identities, enhancing user interactions and experiences. Biometric artistry and emotional intelligence in authentication were discussed as advanced methods of verifying identity based on unique physical or behavioral characteristics and emotional patterns, respectively. Neuro-authentication or brainwave authentication and multisensory authentication represent cutting-edge developments, using neurological patterns or multisensory inputs for verification. The chapter also covered dynamic avatar identities, reflecting the personalization and context-aware aspects of a virtual presence. Furthermore, the chapter covered the growing importance of quantum-resistance encryption and safeguarding identities against emerging threats. Finally, it talked about AI-powered guardians, which use AI to manage and protect identity data dynamically. Overall, the chapter provided coverage of the future identity landscape and highlighted the convergence of technology, security, and user experience as key drivers in the evolution of how you will define and protect your digital self.

CHAPTER 4

The Rise of Biometric Systems

In this chapter, you will explore the history and evolution of biometric systems and how various biometric technologies and applications are used today. Biometrics are unique physical and behavioral characteristics that can be used to identify and verify individuals. Biometric systems can be based on fingerprints, the iris and retina, DNA, gait, etc.

The use of biometric systems has raised a number of important ethical and legal challenges as well as reinforced existing social inequalities, so it is important to be aware of the potential risks of biometric systems before using them.

In this chapter, you will learn about the following:

- The cultural acceptance of biometric systems

- Types of biometric systems

- Biometric system designs

- The Pitfalls of biometrics

Introduction to Biometrics

Biometrics is derived from two words; *bio* means life, and *metrics* means measure. In the technological world, *biometrics* means the automated recognition of individuals based on the human's psychological and behavioral characteristics. Biometrics harness the unique psychological and behavioral traits of individuals to offer an unparalleled layer of security, outpacing traditional passwords, PINs, etc., because biometrics are difficult to forge.

49

© Shivakumar R. Goniwada 2024
S. R. Goniwada, *Introduction to One Digital Identity*, https://doi.org/10.1007/979-8-8688-0255-3_4

There are two types of biometrics.

- Psychological biometrics

- Behavioral biometrics

The psychological biometrics are related to the physical characteristics of an individual such as fingerprints, face shape and features, iris and retina makeup, vein patterns, and DNA.

The behavioral biometrics are related to the behavior or actions of individuals such as how they speak, type, and walk.

Today, biometrics play a pivotal role in myriad sectors, including smartphones, healthcare, cross-border apps, the banking sector, etc. As their prominence grows, so does the imperative for stringent data protection measures, given the sensitivity of the information used. I cover the details of regulations, privacy, and compliance in Chapter 12.

The History and Evolution of Biometric Systems

The term *biometric* first appeared in the 18th century. There was evidence that humans used biometrics to verify individual identities for various purposes including signing legal and business documents with thumb impressions. By the late 18th century, the field of *phrenology* (now regarded as pseudoscience) looked at skull shape as a defining characteristic of an individual.

In the 19th century, Alphonse Bertillon, a criminologist, pioneered a groundbreaking system known as *anthropometry*, which served as a method for criminal identification before the advent of high-tech crime investigation tools. Bertillon's system focused on the precise measurement of various physical attributes such as head length, eye distance, and overall body proportions. Each of these measurements contributed to a detailed and unique identifier for individuals, essentially creating an early form of a biometric profile. This system became a dominant force in criminal identification during that era. Law enforcement agencies and criminal investigators relied on these measurements to differentiate and track individuals involved in criminal activities. This method provided a systematic and standardized way to catalog and document physical characteristics, helping authorities to link individuals to crimes or establish their identities. For decades, this method played a crucial role in the field of criminal investigations; however, it eventually saw a decline with the rise of more advanced forensic techniques, particularly the adoption of fingerprinting.

In the early 20th century, a significant revolution in forensic science occurred with the widespread adoption of fingerprinting, a breakthrough that replaced earlier methods of Bertillon's anthropometry. This transformation was largely attributed to the work of British polymath Sir Francis Galton, who, inspired by Charles Darwin's research on inheritance, delved into the intricate world of fingerprints. Galton studied the unique patterns present in fingerprints, demonstrating their remarkable individuality and permanence. Based on Galton's research, Leonard Darwin became a champion for fingerprinting as a highly accurate and reliable tool for personal identification. The scientific evidence supporting the uniqueness and permanence of fingerprints paved the way for their acceptance as a superior method in criminal investigations. The delicate whorls, loops, and ridges on fingerprints proved to be not only unique but also enduring over time. This made fingerprints an invaluable resource for law enforcement.

In the later 20th century, behavioral biometrics such as voice and keystroke dynamics started to gain traction. These methods are starting to be used in banking, security systems, etc. The late 20th and early 21st centuries are known as the digital age, partly because advancement in technology has catalyzed a surge in varied biometric modalities, such as face recognition, iris and retina scanning, hand and finger geometry, DNA analysis, and gait analysis. Today's biometric systems have become increasingly sophisticated and accurate due to the advancement of technologies and processing power. They are able to identity individuals with a high degree of accuracy, even in challenging climatic conditions. Also, biometric technology has become affordable, which has led to its widespread adoption in a variety of systems.

The following are the biggest biometric implementations in terms of volume:

1. In India, the government has implemented a massive biometric identification program called Aadhaar. Aadhaar has been widely accepted by Indian citizens, as it is made it easier to access government services and financial transactions.

2. In China, the government has used facial recognition technology to monitor and surveil its citizens.

3. In the United States, the U.S. customs and border protection agencies have integrated facial recognition at airports and land borders, processing more than 300 million travelers.

4.   In Europe, the Schengen Area countries use fingerprints and facial recognition at airports and land borders. Also, several countries integrate fingerprints and digital signatures into their ID cards, and fingerprint database and DNA analysis are employed for criminal investigations.

The Art and Aesthetics of Biometrics

Biometric identification based on human aesthetics introduces a unique approach to personal recognition by examining an individual's distinct aesthetic look rather than psychological traits. This is an emerging field of research that explores the possibility of using individual's aesthetic preferences to verify their identity. The aesthetic preferences are influenced by a variety of factors such as culture, personal experience, genes, etc.[1] Researchers have found aesthetic preferences are relatively stable over time and can be used to identify individuals with good accuracy rates. Biometric patterns such as iris, fingerprint, and voice waveform all are unique to each other.

Iris patterns are made up of complex colors and texture. They are formed during fetal development and remain relatively stable throughout an individual's life. No two individuals have exactly the same iris pattern. The art of the iris pattern lies in the intricate details and symmetry.

Fingerprints are also formed during fetal development and remain relatively stable throughout an individual's life. This pattern is also very complex, and no two individuals have exactly the same pattern. The art of the fingerprint is made up of textures and swirling ridges and valleys.

Voice waveforms are sound waves that are produced by human voice and are formed by the vibrations of the vocal cords and the resonating chambers of the head and throat. These patterns are sometimes mimicked, however, and AI algorithms can possibly generate similar waveforms with the same pitch, tones, and timbres. The technology needs to evolve to master identifying unique waveforms.

This type of biometric identification is an upcoming technology with a variety of applications. Online security, personalized products and services, and marketing and advertisement applications could be enabled to use aesthetic preferences.

---

[1] https://www.ncbi.nlm.nih.gov/pmc/articles/PMC7071451/

Cultural Acceptance and Resistance to Biometrics

Biometric technologies are increasingly common across industries. For example, biometrics are extensively used in governmental services, financial services, law enforcement, and healthcare. Some individuals have some concerns about the privacy and security of biometric data, while other individuals worry about the potential discrimination and abuse of the technology.

Culture is a significant factor role in the use of biometric technologies; in some cultures, biometric are seen as a convenient and efficient way to access various services, and in other cultures, biometrics are viewed as suspicious.

Trust plays a pivotal role in how societies perceive and accept biometric verification. The history of surveillance in a country can deeply influence public sentiment, creating heightened levels of skepticism and mistrust. The authorities must build trust with citizens by understanding their concerns and creating a system with transparent, accountable safeguards.

Biometric Technologies

Biometric technologies capture and store unique physiological and behavioral patterns of individuals and then compare those patterns against stored details to verify an identity.

Biometric technologies have varying characteristics suited to different populations, environments, and risk tolerances, and each technology has different strengths and weaknesses. Assessing these factors is key to designing a system that balances user experience.

- On the physiological level are technologies such as fingerprints, in which ridges and valleys are mapped; facial recognition, which measures distinct landmarks on the face; iris scanning, which measures unique patterns in the colored part of the eye; and DNA sequencing, which analyzes the genetic code of an individual.

- On the behavior side, technologies examine the unique way someone signs their name, the rhythm and dynamics of their typing, and their unique way of walking.

The process in both physiological and behavioral biometric tools involves converting these captured details into digital formats and employing algorithms to encode templates. When an individual attempts to access a biometrically secured system, a real-time scan is conducted and compared to the stored template by using artificial intelligence (AI) and machine learning (ML) algorithms.

Psychological Biometrics

Psychological biometrics are a type of biometric that measures and analyzes a person's unique psychological characteristics. There are numerous types of techniques that are used to measure biometrics.

Fingerprint Recognition

Fingerprint recognition is arguably the most enduring biometric technology to date. Over several centuries, the unique pattern of ridges and valleys on fingerprints has been extremely reliable. As the science of fingerprinting has become more refined, it is the de facto standard for identifying and verifying individuals in various use cases across industries.

Fingerprint features are categorized into three levels of detail, each capturing different aspects of the fingerprint's unique structure. The unique features are pattern image, minutiae points, and ridge and pore details.

- The pattern image involves the microscopic structure of the fingerprint. It categorizes fingerprints based on the overall ridge flow and pattern. The unique features of this image are loop, whorl, arch, and tented arch.

- The minutiae points are the microscopic features present in the ridges, and this is where the majority of unique fingerprint details are found. The unique features are the ridge ending, bifurcation, short ridge or island, dot, bridge, delta, and core.

- The ridge and pore details focus on fine-grained details of the ridges. The unique features are the ridge width, ridge shape, ridge edge, and ridge pores.

The pattern and minutiae are sufficient enough in most commercial biometric verification uses, and the ridge and pore are more useful for advanced verification like forensic analysis.

Fingerprint Recognition Process

The fingerprint recognition process consists of different methodologies, from image acquisition to continuous training. Here are the steps:

1. **Image acquisition:** This is the initial step to capture a raw fingerprint image, typically done using optical, capacitive, or ultrasonic sensors. The quality of the image is crucial as the clear image ensures more accurate matching.

2. **Preprocessing:** This step involves improving the quality of the fingerprint image by enhancing the ridge pattern and reducing noise. The techniques used in this step are orientation field estimation, ridge frequency estimation, and image binarization.

3. **Feature extraction:** In this step, the unique features such as minutiae points are extracted, and these features act as the basis for comparison in the last stages.

4. **Postprocessing:** In this phase, any false minutiae or noise introduced during the feature extraction step is removed and refines the extracted features for matching.

5. **Matching:** This step is the core step where the extracted features are compared against what is in the existing database. In the verification process, the fingerprint is matched against a single or preselected template, and in the identification process, it matches against multiple templates for potential matches.

6. **Decision:** In this step, the decision is made based on the matching score generated during the matching step. If the score is in predetermined threshold, the fingerprint is considered as matching.

7. **Training:** In this step, the algorithm is continuously learning, so the system adapts and updates its templates based on the newly encountered variations of the fingerprint.

Fingerprint Quality Control

The quality of the fingerprint images is crucial for accurate recognition. Poor-quality images can lead to false positive, false negatives, or inconclusive results. To ensure high-quality fingerprint images, it is important to follow rigorous quality control.

The following are the key quality checks that you need to consider:

1. **Resolution check:** The image must have a sufficient resolution; the measurement of a fingerprint is usually in dots per inch (DPI). According to industry standards, the standard resolution of many fingerprints system is 500 DPI.

2. **Contract and brightness:** The image should have a good balance of contrast and brightness; the ridges should clearly be distinguishable from the valleys.

3. **Ridge definition:** The ridges should be continuous and well-defined. Faint ridge patterns can be inaccurate during feature extraction.

4. **Noise reduction:** The image should be free from artifacts and noise, which can be caused by dirt, smudges, or scars on a finger.

5. **Coverage:** The entire central region of the fingerprint must be covered because it contains the unique features.

6. **Slippage detection:** If the finger moves or slips during the process, it can create distortion.

Along with the quality checks, you must follow the standards defined by the International Association for Identification (IAI). [2]

---

[2] https://www.theiai.org/

Matching Algorithms

The matching algorithms play a crucial role in determining the similarity between the fingerprint at registration time and the authentication verification. Depending on the modality, different algorithms and techniques are used. The matching algorithms are based on the premise of the types of correlations, minutiae, and ridge feature.

A *correlation* is a measure of the similarity between two fingerprint images. The following are a few matching correlation types:

1. **Linear correlations:** In this method, the templates (registration and verification) are directly compared using Pearson's correlation co-efficient. Pearson's method is a statistical measure of the linear correlation between two variables. It ranges from -1 and 1, with a value of 0 indicating no correlation. With the use of Pearson's method in fingerprint matching, a high positive correlation would suggest an exact match between the registration and verification templates.

2. **Cross-correlation:** This correlation matching algorithm can be used to measure the similarity between two fingerprint images when either template is shifted relative to each other. This type of matching is useful when the templates might be out of sync due to timing or alignment differences.

3. **Phase correlation:** The phase correlation matching algorithm can be used to measure the similarities between the phase spectra of images by using the Fourier transform method. The Fourier transform is a mathematical operation that decomposes a function into its constituent frequencies and can be used to perform various tasks such as removing noise and distortions, so the phase correlation uses this equation to identify translation shifts between two images.

4. **Normalized cross-correlation:** This method uses the variation of cross-correlation where the templates are normalized before calculating the correlation. This method provides more robust matches when there are variations in brightness.

5. **Coefficient of determination (R-squared):** This method is a statistical measure of the accuracy of the fingerprint system. R-squared is a range from 0 to 1. 0 is an independent variable that indicates the images does not provide any variance, and 1 indicates matching perfectly with the templates. It can measure the fit of the model data, but it does not consider other factors such as the quality of data or the design of the biometric system.

Minutiae matching is used to determine whether minutiae extracted from the fingerprint matches the template. There are two methodologies used in minutiae matching. They are as follows:

6. **Global minutiae matching:** In this matching algorithm, the spatial layout and relationship between all the minutiae of a fingerprint are assessed. This algorithm compares the registration and verification templates with the distance and angles between these two minutiae points.

7. **Local minutiae matching:** This algorithm focuses on certain aspects of specific regions instead of the entire fingerprint. Instead of evaluating the whole minutiae, it centers around the primary minutiae and its immediate neighbors.

Ridge feature matching goes beyond the minutiae points and considers other inherent features. This can be used when the minutiae points are poor quality.

Facial Recognition

Facial recognition relies on the physical features of the face that are determined by genetics. These features include the shape of the eyes, nose, mouth, and chin, as well as the distance between these facial features. Facial recognition is widely used in law enforcement.

Facial recognition stands out in the realm of biometric technologies, primarily because of its noncontact nature compared to fingerprint and iris scanners. However, facial features can vary depending on the individual's age, gender, ethnicity, expression, and lightning conditions.

Facial Recognition Process

The facial recognition process is a two-step approach. The first step is to capture and extract facial features, and the second step is the recognition process.

In the capturing process, you need a high-resolution camera with infrared or depth sensors to capture raw images of the face. This process has lots of challenges, such as a face's dynamic nature. Various angles, expressions, lightning conditions, external features like eyewear, hats, etc., and makeup can add variability to the captured raw image of the face.

The recognition approach ensures the advanced algorithms map out the distinct facial landmarks and extract features, creating a unique facial signature. This signature is compared against the registration signature for identification and verification. Deep learning and neural networks have further enhanced the accuracy and speed of the recognition process.

Facial Quality Control

The International Committee for Information Technology Standards (INCITS) has set a few guidelines for facial images. These guidelines are as follows:

1. **Resolution:** The image must have a resolution of 100 pixels per inch (ppi) at a distance of 1 meter. The pixels are between the eye centers to capture the detailed facial features.

2. **Lighting:** The image must be fit well and be evenly illuminated, and direct light from the front is recommended with no strong light from behind.

3. **Pose:** The face should be posed directly in front of the camera with minimal tilt to ensure uniform recognition.

4. **Expression:** The face should have a natural expression, and the eyes should be open and looking at the camera; extreme facial expressions can distort features.

5. **Occlusion:** The face should not be obscured by glasses, a hat, a mask, or anything else.

6. **Digital alterations:** The raw image should not be digitally altered or retouched to maintain the authenticity of the facial features.

If you are using a 3D facial recognition system, then a few additional guidelines need to be considered to ensure accuracy and effectiveness.

7. Ensure the environment is conducive to 3D data collection as 3D systems are less sensitive to lightning variations, but extreme conditions still affect the image capture.

8. Implement algorithms to detect attempts at spoofing, such as using 3D masks.

9. 3D data is more voluminous than 2D data; ensure you have more storage space.

Matching Algorithms

The facial recognition techniques are broadly classified into two categories.

- Appearance-based methods
- Model-based techniques

Appearance-Based Methods

This technique is based on the concept of analyzing the holistic appearance of the face. The following are some algorithms:

1. **Eigenfaces:** This method uses principal component analysis (PCA) to represent the whole face as a linear combination of the principal component derived from the covariance matrix of the training set. PCA is a widely used statistical technique for dimensionality reduction.

2. **Fisherfaces:** This method uses linear discriminant analysis (LDA) to maximize between-class scatter while minimizing within-class scatter, which means face features are normally distributed.

3. **Deep learning and neural networks:** These algorithms are used to train the model to recognize faces.

Model-Based Methods

This method focuses on creating a 2D or 3D model of the face and then using that model to identify an individual. These are two algorithms used in this method:

1. **Active appearance model (AAM):** This statistical model captures the shape and texture variation of the 2D or 3D shape of the face. This method is trained on a set of known face images and then used to generate new face models.

2. **3D morphable models:** This method uses 3D data to generate a model of the face. It combines the shape and texture information from 3D scans of individuals and creates a morphable model that can be adjusted to fit new faces.

Overall, the appearance-based methods are computationally more efficient than model-based methods, but accuracy is less in challenging conditions with light, shadow, etc. Model-based methods are more accurate in challenging conditions.

Iris and Retinal Scanning

Of all the biometrics available today other than DNA, the retina and iris hold the most distinctive data for identifying and verifying an individual. The retina is a layer of tissue at the back of the eye that contains photoreceptor cells that convert light into electrical signals that are transmitted to the brain. The iris is the colored part of the eye that surrounds the pupil. Both retina and iris have unique patterns that can be used to identify individuals. Retinal scanning is a noninvasive biometric technology that uses a low-powered beam of light to create a digital image of the retina. Iris recognition is also a noninvasive biometric technology that uses a camera to capture an image of the iris. Both retinal and iris recognition are highly accurate biometric identification technologies; however, retinal scanning is generally considered to be more accurate than iris scanning.

Retinal and Iris Recognition Process

The advancements in iris and retina recognition technology are driven by both hardware and software. Here are the steps for the recognition process:

1. The iris recognition system uses high-resolution cameras equipped with specialized infrared illumination. This infrared light highlights the unique features of the iris.

2. New cameras are built with adaptive focus capabilities. This helps to adjust automatically from far distances.

3. The process uses advanced algorithms to stabilize image capture in real time like in motion.

4. Once the image is captured, there are several preprocessing steps to be carried out including image enhancement, normalization, noise reduction, etc.

5. After preprocessing, algorithms are used to identify unique patterns in the iris for ridges, do furrows analysis, convert it into a compact digital representation called iris code, and store it in the highly secured storage medium.

Matching Algorithms

Iris and retina scanning uses a variety of advanced algorithms to compare the iris codes of registration and verification. The most common algorithms are Hamming distance and normalized Hamming distance.

The Hamming distance measures the number of different bits of two binary strings. If two iris codes have a low Hamming distance, it indicates a high similarity, and the normalized Hamming distance identifies the distance by the length of two strings.

In addition to these algorithms, various algorithms are available, but they all use the iris patterns, such as ridges and furrows, and the textual information of the iris.

DNA Matching

DNA profiling is used to identify individuals based on their unique DNA profiles. The profiling method uses short tandem repeats (STRs) and variable number tandem repeats (VNTRs) to analyze specific regions of the genome that have repetitive sequences. The STRs are short sequences of DNA that are repeated multiple times in a row, and the VNTRs vary from person to person.

The DNA profiling is performed by extracting DNA samples such as blood, saliva, or semen and amplifying it using a technique called *polymerase chain reaction* (PCR). PCR produces millions of copies of the DNA, which makes it easier to detect.

After extracting the samples, the scientist focuses on specific regions or loci on the chromosomes. The loci contains STRs that are unique to each individuals. By counting the number of repeats at each locus, a unique DNA profile for an individual can be established.

After creating the profiles, there are three distinctive results: exclusion, nonexclusion, and no result.

Exclusion is the definitive result if the DNA profile of the registration does not match the verification DNA. Nonexclusion is when the DNA profile matches the profiles, and no result is due to various reasons such as a degraded sample, contamination, or insufficient DNA.

Behavioral Biometrics

Behavioral biometrics examine the unique way someone signs their name, the rhythm and dynamics of their typing, or their unique way of walking.

Gait Recognition

Gait recognition focuses on the dynamic, repetitive manner in which an individual moves. Movement is different for each person, encompassing a blend of acquired habits and innate psychological features. The gait in biometrics is a passive nature as individuals need not actively participate or even be aware of being measured, as their walking pattern can be captured from a distance. The algorithms dissect this visual data and translate the sway of the hips, the length of a stride, or the rhythm of footsteps into a unique identifier. However, you need to carefully look into factors such as footwear, pace alterations, and temporary physical ailments that can introduce variance.

Gait Recognition Process

Gait recognition establishes a unique movement-based identifier for individuals and uses the static and dynamic approaches for recognition process.

1. The static shape approach is based on analyzing the visual silhouette of an individual as they walk; these images are captured typically by the use of CCTV or specialized cameras. The frame extracts the walking pattern of an individual and filters out unnecessary background details and other potential distractions. Once isolated, the silhouette is processed through subsequent iteration, and a series of distinct images is generated. These individually processed images collectively form the gait signature, which is unique to each individual.

2. The dynamic shape approach is not about the static images but captures the physical movement of the walking person. This follows the approach of an accelerometer, a device sensitive to motion and velocity changes. To capture the intricate details, the accelerometer is strategically placed in an individual's leg. As the individual walks, the device records the movement dynamics such as vertical, forward-backing, and side-to-side. The output of this device provides a person's stride mechanism, and the system can deduce the unique signature of an individual.

Gait Analysis

After the image captured, this process involves translating the raw data into a set of identifiable and unique characteristics. There are two analysis process you can use; they are model-based analysis and holistic analysis.

1. Model-based analysis works by splitting the walking pattern into quantifiable metrics and relative relationships made up of the distance between the head and pelvis and the distance from the pelvis to the feet. Once the process identifies a metric, it focuses on the dynamics of the movement, such as the distance between the moving feet, which can be crucial in determining the specifics of an individual's gait. Along with these measurements, this model analyzes the angles formed while walking. At the end, it collects both distances and angles and then converts them to vectors. These form the representation of the individual's gait.

2. Holistic analysis focuses on the entire silhouette of an individual walking instead of specific metrics. This model identifies the unique features from the overall walking pattern like how the body moves and flows while walking.

Overall, the model-based approach is more accurate than holistic analysis, but it is more complex and computationally expensive. In addition, you can use deep learning, machine learning, and statistical analysis to analyze the gait features.

Gait Templates

Once the gait features are analyzed, then you need to create a biometric template, which is critical for recognizing the gait. Unlike other biometric comparisons, the gait is based on a dynamic sequence of movements. There are several techniques available for the templates and the matching process; the most specific ones are direct matching, dynamic time wrapping, and hidden Markov methods.

1. *Direct matching* is a simple method where the captured gait sequence is directly compared with reference data. This technique uses metrics such as the distance between data points.

2. *The dynamic time wrapping algorithm* works by measuring the similarity between two temporal sequences, which may vary in speed or time. It compares the two gait sequences that might be out of sync or at different speeds. It wraps the time axis of the sequences to align them optimally by facilitating a more effective comparison.

3. *The hidden Markov method* is a statistical model that assesses the probability of a sequence of observed events like shapes or movements based on the underlying, unobserved states. It predicts the likelihood of a particular walking sequence based on the observed strides of the current steps and the probability of subsequent steps.

The best method depends on the specific application. Dynamic time wrapping and hidden Markov methods both provide good accuracy.

Hand Geometry Recognition

Hand geometry focuses on the distinct physical structure of an individual's hand, not on intricate details like fingerprints. The uniqueness of this recognition type is that it is based on the hand's shape with attributes such as finger length, palm width, and distance between joints. These attributes provide a certain level of distinctiveness, but they don't provide granularity like fingerprints or retinas do. So, hand geometry is seldom used in large-scale identification scenarios where the goal is to pinpoint an individual's identity among millions of individuals. Hand geometry is used primarily for verification where the objective is to confirm a person's claimed identity.

A hand geometry scanner employs prisms and light-emitting diodes (LEDs) to capture raw images of both the back of the hand and the palm for rendering a 2D depiction of the hand. For 3D images, the scanner uses five guiding pegs beneath the camera. While the pegs aid in hand positioning, they introduce a complication that adds noise to the data.

Once the image is captured and processed, the system measures the specific attributes of the hand and calculates the average measurement of attributes to create a template and a compact binary mathematical file.

One of the main challenges of hand geometry is that many geometric features of the hand can be correlated or similar between people. This similarity can impede the extraction of unique features.

Voice Recognition

Voice recognition is unique in the contemporary biometrics landscape in that it straddles both behavioral and physical biometrics because it is based on both the physical characteristics of the vocal tract and the behavioral pattern of the speaker. The physical characteristics of the vocal tract such as the shape of the mouth and the length of the vocal chords affect the pitch and tone of the voice. The behavioral pattern such as rate of speech and emphasis on certain words also affects the sound of the voice.

Voice recognition technology has improved significantly in recent years and now is able to identify and verify individuals with high accuracy.

Voice recognition is a mix of physical, biology, and technology, and it delves into the intricate nuances of sound production to identify individuals. Sound production is initiated at the vocal cords. When communication is intended, muscles governing these cords contract, reducing the gap between them. However, the voice uniqueness is sculpted as this sound wave travels through the vocal tract, and as sound travels, it forms a distinct pattern for individuals.

Consistency in the medium of voice capture is pivotal for the effectiveness of a voice recognition system. The process relies on the nuances and subtleties of voice patterns, which can be affected by the device used for recording. The quality and limitations of each device can introduce slight variations in the voice samples, which might significantly influence recognition accuracy. Beyond device quality, several other factors include emotional state, medium inconsistency, physical conditions, and environmental factors.

Voice Analysis

Voice analysis relies on computational and statistical methods to decode the uniqueness embedded in each individual's voice. After capturing the voice samples, the subsequent stages involve extracting unique features from this sample and then creating a template that serves as a reference for future comparisons. This process uses algorithms and statistical models to understand the complexities of human speech.

1. **Hidden Markov model (HMM):** This is a statistical model that is used with text-dependent systems; it requires individuals to speak a specific phrase or sentence in order to be identified. It is able to model the changes and fluctuations of the voice over time.

2. **Gaussian mixture model (GMM):** This is a state mapping model that is used with text-independent systems and that allows individuals to speak any phrase to be identified. This algorithm is able to model unique sound characteristics of an individual's voice.

Both have their strengths and are employed based on specific requirements and constraints. HMMs focus on the sequence and progression of speech, and GMMs provide a robust statistical representation of the unique voice features. By using a hybrid approach with both algorithms, you can achieve the best recognition performance.

Keystroke Dynamics

Keystroke recognition is a behavioral biometric that uses the unique way in which an individual types to identify the person. This system typically measures the timing, pressure, and rhythm of an individual's keystrokes. The rhythm isn't just the speed of typing; it is about the duration of how long the keys are held down, the force applied, the intervals between successive keystrokes, and the overall sequence of key presses. Such nuances in typing behavior craft a distinctive signature for every individual.

Keystroke Process

The keystroke enrollment and verification process involves typing a specific word or a group of words multiple times. The same words or group of words must be used during both the enrollment and verification processes to ensure that the behavioral typing of individuals is consistent. The enrollment process creates a template that consists of specific words or a group of words to be typed multiple times. The enrollment process involves multiple sessions to create a more consistent behavioral pattern capture.

The statistical correlation between the enrollment and verification templates is used to identify or verify the individual, and it is a relatively noninvasive biometric technology. A keystroke recognition system can be used to identify individuals without requiring them to touch any special hardware or software.

Keystroke dynamics are a delicate blend of behavioral biometrics and statistical modeling. This biometric offers a unique form of authentication, but its efficiency rests on the precision of the enrollment process.

Biometric System Design

The biometric architecture is a blend of hardware and software technologies. The exterior biometric system is hardware, and the underlying mechanism is software with a set of advanced engineering and algorithmic components, as shown in Figure 4-1.

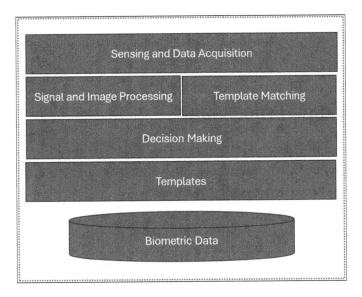

Figure 4-1. *Biometric design*

Sensing and Data Acquisition

Sensing and data acquisition is pivotal in the biometric process; it is the foundation upon which all other subcomponents rely. Ensuring the accurate and consistent capture of biometric data is crucial as it is directly impacts the system's overall effectiveness and reliability. This component is further categorized into the following steps:

1. **Raw data capture and extraction:** This initial step involves capturing an individual's raw data. This could be a fingerprint, a facial scan, an iris and retina scan, etc., depending on what biometric system you are using.

2. **Conversion for processing:** After the initial capture of raw data, the data must be converted into a format suitable for processing. In this step, the raw data is converted into the digital format that can be analyzed by the biometric system.

3. **Enrollment data:** This step collects the data for registration or enrollment time; the system uses this data to create an enrollment template and store it.

4. **Verification and identification data:** This step collects the live data that compares it against the enrollment template to confirm the user's identity.

Signal and Image Processing

The signal and image processing component is a vital step in the biometric recognition process. This component turns raw sensor data into actionable biometric templates. There are various substeps involved in this component.

Preprocessing the Biometric Raw Image

This step captures raw biometric data for feature extraction by processing noise reduction, normalization across images, and alignment of the image. This phase consists of subprocesses such as detection, alignment, segmentation, and normalization.

1. **Detection:** This subphase determines the type of biometric signal present in the captured data stream derived from the raw biometric image. This is essential for recognizing the physiological or behavioral trait consistently and voluntarily presented to the sensor.

2. **Alignment:** This is the process of establishing the correct orientation and centering of the biometric raw image. This accounts for any variations in rotation, ensuring accurate feature capture and improving the quality of subsequent templates for enrollment and verification.

3. **Segmentation:** This is the extraction of the biometric signal of interest from the acquired data system. Before segmentation, successful detection is necessary to confirm the presence of relevant data in the raw image. Extraneous data is then cropped out during segmentation, focusing only on the areas containing the detected signal.

4. **Normalization:** This involves adjusting or scaling the relevant biometric data discovered during segmentation. This ensures that the data is within a predetermined range of acceptable values. The normalization serves two primary purposes, such as energy-level normalization and scale normalization.

Quality Control Checks

The quality control in this, particularly for biometric systems, is a crucial phase ensuring the accuracy and reliability of the biometric identification or verification. It involves several components, each addressing different aspects of quality assurance. These components constantly assess, predict, and improve the quality of the biometric data being processed. This not only enhances the performance of the biometric system but also ensures that it remains robust against errors.

1. **Feedback loop:** This component ensures the immediate detection of any flaws in the captured biometric signal. If a low-quality signal is detected, the system triggers a feedback loop, prompting the end user to resubmit their biometric trait. This is particularly useful for noncooperative users who may need to present their biometric data multiple times because of various issues such as poor positioning or low-quality captures. This process ensures that only high-quality, reliable data enters the system, reducing the likelihood of false matches or nonmatches due to poor data quality.

2. **Predictive mechanism:** This component gauges how well two biometric templates (enrollment and verification) will match. This component calculates quality scores, which serve multiple purposes.

   • Determining if the signal data is sufficient for a successful match

   • Indicating the level of signals and image processing required

   • Formulating specific matching strategies

   • Measuring if enough unique features are extracted for quality enrollment and verification templates

   This predictive approach optimizes the matching process, tailoring it according to the quality of the input, and helps in strategizing the biometric verification mechanism.

3. **Input mechanism in multimodel biometric solutions:** In multimodal biometric systems, quality control scores are critical for integrating and optimizing various biometric modalities like

fingerprint, facial, iris recognition, etc. It involves using quality scores to assign different weighted values in the signal and image subphase for various biometric modalities. This ensures that each modality contributes effectively to the overall decision of the system based on the quality of data it provides. This component helps in harmonizing and enhancing the overall performance of multimodal biometric systems.

Raw Image Enhancement

This step improves the clarity and visibility of features in the biometric data; it uses techniques such as histogram equalization, ridge enhancement, or sharpening details. The focus is on refining the raw biometric image to ensure that it's in the best possible form for the subsequent creation of the enrollment and verification templates. This steps involves multiple substeps for enhancement purposes.

1. **Replacement of unreadable features:** This step eliminates noise and unclear areas that might lead to errors in feature extraction. The point of this step is to identify and mark the unreadable or low-quality features of the biometric image. These areas are then replaced with blank spots or neutral data. By doing so, the system ensures that only clean, distinct, and accurate features are considered for template creation. The benefit of this step is to reduce the likelihood of errors during feature extraction by ensuring that the data used to create templates is of high quality and reliable.

2. **Simplification of complex features:** This steps reduces the complexity of the biometric image for more efficient processing. It analyzes the biometric image and identifies areas that are overly complex or detailed. These areas are then simplified using various image processing techniques. The aim is to maintain the essential characteristics of these features while reducing their complexity to facilitate easier and faster processing. This steps simplifies the complex parts of the biometric image and makes it easier for the system to process and analyze the image, leading to faster and more accurate biometric recognition.

3. **Fixing and repairing damaged or missing features:** This step reconstructs repair parts of the biometric image that are damaged or missing. This component involves the extrapolation and estimation of missing or damaged features based on the analysis of adjacent, reliable features through techniques like interpolation, and morphological operations. Fixing these elements ensures that the final template is as complete and accurate as possible.

Unique Feature Extraction

This step captures the distinct characteristics of the data that differentiates individuals. For example, in fingerprint data, this involves identifying minutiae points like ridge endings or bifurcation, and in facial recognition, it identifies the position and shape of the eyes, nose, and mouth. The entire feature extraction process is a delicate balance of time and accuracy. Ideally, the system must spend enough time analyzing the biometric raw image to ensure distinctiveness and uniqueness. This step consists of multiple subprocesses that help you to extract features.

1. **Unique feature location and determination:** This step identifies distinct elements in a biometric sample that can differentiate one individual from another. The process is to examine the biometric raw image to locate unique features. For instance, in fingerprints, this could involve identifying minutiae points within the ridges and valleys; in iris recognition, it locates unique patterns like furrows, coronas, and freckles.

2. **Extraction of the unique features:** This step isolates and captures the identified unique features from the biometric data. Once the unique feature is located, the algorithm extracts the features and typically converts them into a format that a computer can process, understand, and compare.

3. **Development and creation of enrollment templates:** This step creates a database of templates against which future biometric samples can be compared. The extracted features are compiled into a comprehensive enrollment template. This template is essentially a mathematical or statistical representation of the individual's unique biometric features.

4. **Behavior model creation:** This step accommodates behavioral biometrics like signature or keystroke recognition. It creates a statistical model based on the dynamic biometric data. This data is different from physical biometrics because the patterns are behavioral and change over time.

Postprocessing of the Unique Features

This step is to optimize the extracted data and remove any redundant or irrelevant data, further enhancing specific features or converting the feature data into a standardized format suitable for comparison. This is crucial for refining the extracted data and managing biometric raw data. This step involves multiple substeps to manage the postprocessing of data.

- **Refining extracted unique features:** This ensures the extracted features are optimally prepared for the final matching process. During this process, the system examines the unique features extracted during the future extraction. It looks for any grouping or cluster of features that might have inadvertently formed. Such groupings can cause errors and increase processing time during the matching phase.

- **Managing biometric raw images:** Once the unique features have been extracted and refined, the system must decide what to do with the original biometric raw image. Typically, it is either archived for future reference or discarded to free up storage space and maintain privacy.

- **Optimizing for future processing:** This ensures that the data is in the best possible form for future comparisons and can be easily accessed or matched against new biometric samples.

Template Matching

The template matching component makes a vital decision that grants or denies access to users. The matching process is complex and uses the laws of statistics and probability to determine a match. There are four types of matching: verification matching, identification matching, vector matching, and cohort matching.

- *Verification matching* is a type of matching that verifies the identity of an individual who is already known to the system. An example is using a fingerprint scanner in an office to unlock the phone.

- *Identification matching* is a type of matching that verifies the identity of an individual who is not known to the system, for example, using a scanner to identify a robber.

- *Vector matching* is a type of matching that compares the enrollment template directly to the verification template.

- *Cohort matching* compares the verification template to a subset of enrollment templates that are similar to the verification template.

The matching component can either search the entire database of enrollment templates or use the winnowing or binning technique to search a database.

- The *winnowing technique* reduces the number of comparisons made during a database search. Instead of comparing a sample against every template in a database, the system narrows the search to a smaller subset, making the process faster and more efficient. This technique uses the filtering and indexing methods to search a database.

- The *binning technique* segments biometric templates into smaller, more manageable categories of bins based on the features or criteria. The criteria is based on the metadata such as the date of enrollment, etc.

Decision-Making

The decision-making component compares the matching score to the security threshold and decides whether to authenticate or identify the individual. There are two ways you can make decisions.

- Threshold automatic-based decision

- Administrative decision

In the threshold decision-making, the threshold is used for a match to be declared. The threshold is typically set based on the criticality of the system and can be adjusted regularly by the administrators. There are three type of thresholds.

- **Static threshold:** The static or fixed threshold is used for all verification and identification purposes.

- **Dynamic threshold:** The threshold is adjusted based on the quality of the biometric data and level of security required and is based on where the biometric verification is placed.

- **Individual threshold:** This sets different thresholds for the group of individuals.

The decision component can use a variety of methods to compare the matching score to the security threshold and make a decision; some are threshold based, and some are rank based.

In the administrative decision, the command-and-control center of the biometric system ensures the system functions optimally. In this process, the system administrator configures the threshold and verifies the individual's authentication.

Philosophical Musings: Do We Own Our Data?

The question of whether we own our own data is a complex one. At its core, the data you generate, be it your browsing habits, personal preferences, or even daily routines, is innately intertwined with your identity, maybe leading you believe that it's deeply personal and should remain private. This expectation of privacy stands in stark contrast to the current digital paradigm, where your interactions with online platforms involve an implicit exchange. You get use services for free, and in return they gather and monetize your data. Many of these online platforms argue that once you use their services and provide consent to their terms, any data collected is theirs to use, often for targeted advertising or marketing.

The recent wave of decentralization with blockchain and distributed ledger tech stacks offers a beacon of hope in the quest of personal data ownership. Instead of housing data in monolithic servers under the control of singular entities, decentralization scatters it across a wide network of individual nodes. This not only ensures greater security and resistance against breaches but also hands back the reins of data control to individuals. In essence, every user becomes their own data manager, deciding who gets access to what information. By bypassing intermediaries and empowering individuals with direct ownership and control, decentralization is paving the way for a future where personal data sovereignty isn't just a dream but a tangible reality. I have dedicated Chapter 5 to decentralized identities.

Where Biometrics Can Go Wrong

Biometric systems are not devoid of challenges. A major concern is the realm of privacy and data protection. Engaging with biometrics means handing over highly personal information intricately woven into your digital identity. Without stringent protection measures, the biometric data is susceptible to breaches, posing significant threats if it falls into the wrong hands. Further negative effects are potential biases and inaccuracies. Some biometric systems have shown biases against specific demographics, including women and people of color, leading to skewed results. In addition, biometrics are not always accurate enough to verify authentication due to various factors. Sweat, dirt, and even lightning can affect a system's precision.

Some biometrics systems are vulnerable and expose data to hackers easily. Also, biometric systems could inadvertently lay the foundation for a surveillance society, with potential misuses by authorities further exacerbating mistrust in certain countries.

It is important to weigh the risks and benefits of biometric systems before using them. Biometric systems are excellent for security purposes, but it is important to take steps to protect privacy and prevent misuse.

You need strong data protection for storing and transmitting data, transparency, and accountability with clear policies and procedures. Administrators must have control over the biometric system and must ensure regular audits and oversight of biometric systems to mitigate risks.

The Future of Biometrics: Trends and Predictions

Biometric systems are poised to intertwine more deeply into your daily experience. The symbiosis between biometrics and emerging technologies such as IoT, AR/VR, the metaverse, and AI will redefine how we interact with the digital realm. For instance, the sprawling network of IoT devices, from smart home systems to wearables, might leverage biometrics for seamless authentication, enhancing both security and convenience. Augmented and virtual realities in a repositioning of the entertainment industry could integrate with biometrics to offer better user experiences.

Innovations in biometrics include emotion-based biometrics where a device can detect and respond to an individual's emotional state. Brainwave patterns are also being explored as a biometric measure for a better user experience and security of systems.

Biometrics Security

Usually biometric systems offer a high level of security due to inherent reliance on unique physiological or behavioral attributes, but these systems are not immune to vulnerabilities as these systems can experience various attacks.

- **Spoofing attack:** This type of attack uses fake biometric data to fool the sensor into thinking that it is authenticating or identifying the real person. It can be through a photograph, a video, or facial or fingerprint recognition.

- **Replay attack:** This attack gains access by using previously captured biometric data.

- **Database attack:** This attack gains access to databases to alter templates and other biometric data.

- **Brute-force attack:** This attack uses automated repeated attempts with various biometric inputs to gain unauthorized access.

- **Presentation attack:** This presents the sensor with a biometric sample from someone other than the intended user; for example, the attacker can hold someone's photo or fingerprint image.

You cannot entirely avoid attacks, but you can mitigate these attacks by using the following mitigation procedures:

- **Liveness detection:** This mitigation step is to detect the liveness of the object. For example, you can implement a sensor to detect the liveness of the individual's finger.

- **Encryption:** Ensure biometric data at rest and transit is encrypted to prevent unauthorized access.

- **Template protection:** You can use biometric salting and biohashing to ensure that even if data is stolen, it remains useless without the correct decryption key or algorithm.

To measure a performance of the biometric system, you need to implement measurement metrics.

- **False acceptance rate (FAR):** This metric provides you with the number of times the system incorrectly authorized an unauthorized individual.

- **False rejection rate (FRR):** This metric provides you with the number of times the system wrongly denied access to an authorized individual.

- **Equal error rate (ERR):** This is the point where FAR and FRR are equal.

- **Success rate:** This is the number of genuine attempts that have been correctly authenticated.

- **Failure to enroll rate (FTER):** This metric provides you with the number of times that an individual's biometric data fails to enroll in the system initially.

Summary

The chapter began with an introduction to biometrics, providing an overview of biometric identification methods and their growing importance in security and personal identification. Next it delved into how biometrics integrate with human perception and design, influencing user interaction. The next section explored the societal implications, ethical considerations, and public attitude toward biometric technology. We looked at types of biometrics like fingerprints, facial recognition, iris scan, gait analysis, etc., and discussed their mechanisms and applications. I also explained how you can design a biometric system. Finally, I touched on the ethical and philosophical issues around data ownership and privacy, as well as potential failures, errors, and security breaches in biometric systems.

CHAPTER 5

Decentralized Digital Identity

The importance of secure and private identity management cannot be overstated. Identity data breaches have had far-reaching consequences, impacting people's social connections, professional lives, and financial well-being. In recognition of these challenges, there is growing commitment from the industry to ensure that every individual has the right to own and control their personal digital identity.

This chapter covers the following topics:

- Introduction to decentralization

- Challenges of decentralized digital identities

- The role of blockchain technology in decentralization

- How a decentralized digital identity works

- Standards and specifications available for digital identities

The New Paradigm of Identity

A decentralized identity (DID) is a new paradigm for managing digital identities. Instead of relying on centralized identities such as tech companies and governments to verify and manage personal data, a decentralized identity empowers you to take control of your own data. This self-sovereignty identity ensures that you are the sole authority over your identity, providing both privacy and security advantages.

© Shivakumar R. Goniwada 2024
S. R. Goniwada, *Introduction to One Digital Identity*, https://doi.org/10.1007/979-8-8688-0255-3_5

The underlying mechanism of a DID is blockchain technology. The blockchain's immutable and decentralized characteristics make it helpful for DIDs. Within a blockchain, digital identifiers are created to represent individuals or entities. These identifiers do not disclose personal data on the chain but can be used to validate and verify information on the chain.

These are the steps for implementing a DID:

1. Create a digital identity in a user agent (a user interface application), which gets a unique identifier on the blockchain.

2. Verify the identity from a trusted source such as a bank, government, or affiliated university.

3. Verify the identity from the blockchain without seeing the details of the identity owner.

4. Manage the digital identity, controlling who has access to the information.

Why do we want to shift from centralized systems managed by big tech companies? The answer is that centralized systems are generally controlled by service providers such as Google, Meta, and Apple. This means you have to trust these big organizations blindly, and unfortunately, they can misuse your data with respect to monetization, privacy, and more. A DID places the power of data control back into the hands of individuals.

There are numerous reasons why individuals should want to shift from a centralized system to a decentralized system; the following are a few:

- **Sovereignty:** One of the fundamental principles of DIDs is self-sovereignty. This means you have full control and ownership of your identity without relying on external service providers. This paradigm shift empowers users, ensuring they are not tied to any particular service provider such as Google, Apple, or Meta.

- **Censorship resistance:** Centralized systems often can control, manipulate, or even deny access to your identity or associated services. For example, most platforms depend on Google services for user identification. If you don't want to have Google account, these platforms deny service to you. Decentralized systems by nature are designed to be censor-resistant, ensuring everyone has access to and can control their identity.

- **Interoperability:** A decentralized identity system works on standard protocols; these protocols define how DIDs are created, managed, and used, which means the identity can be seamlessly integrated across various platforms and services.

- **Intermediaries:** Centralized systems require some intermediaries, but DIDs eliminate or reduce the involvement of the number of intermediaries.

- **Trust:** Trust in centralized systems has been eroding for various reasons over the years, from data breaches to the misuse of personal data. Decentralized systems offer a trustless environment where transactions and identity verification are secured by cryptography and consensus mechanisms.

- **Decentralized verifiability:** In a DID system, verification is not reliant on trusting a single centralized authority but is instead based on network consensus. This ensures that any verification, such as credentials or attestation, is universally verifiable across the network without needing to trust a single entity.

Given these reasons and with the advancement of technology, the shift toward decentralized identity systems seems both logical and beneficial for users and organizations. However, shifting toward decentralized identities is not simple; decentralization has its own challenges and complexities for implementation as well as adoption.

Self-Sovereign Identities

A *self-sovereign identity* (SSI) is a new ecosystem to manage a digital identity where you have full control and ownership of your identity. The DID is a fundamental component of the SSI ecosystem, where a unique identifier is used to retrieve DID documents that contain public keys, service endpoints, and other attributes.

The SSI ecosystem is built upon a decentralized architecture, primarily leveraging distributed ledger technology (DLT). At the core of the SSI ecosystem, the DIDs are associated with globally unique, persistent, and cryptographically verifiable identifiers. These DIDs are registered with the SSI system to ensure immutability and tamper resistance. Every DID associated with a DID document is stored on the DLT. The DID document consists of metadata such as public keys, authentication protocols, and service endpoints. The entire SSI ecosystem is based on a cryptographic model. Users of a DID maintain a private key, which is kept confidential, and a public key shared in the DID document. To authenticate or interact within the ecosystem, you sign a transaction using your private keys that can be verified by others using the corresponding public keys. These are digitally attested and cryptographically signed by a trusted entity such as your enterprise organization or some third party such as the government or a bank.

SSI Principles

Every SSI ecosystem is designed based on these principles:

- **Principle of existence:** The existence principle emphasizes the inherent value of an individual's identity. Every human by virtue of being born possesses an inherent identity. This principle in SSI delves deeper to say that an individual identity is not something that can be given or taken away by an external authority. It asserts that every individual's identity is innate and stands independently by external validation or recognition.

- **Principle of control:** This principle empowers you with autonomy over your digital identities and envisions a digital landscape where you are not a passive participant but rather an active custodian of your own data. In the centralized system, you do not have control over your identity; in fact, sometimes it is difficult to remove your identity from the system. However, SSI flips this to give control to you for modification, deletion, etc.

- **Principle of access:** This principle in SSI provides the right to own your data and asserts that individuals should be able to engage with it actively. This includes not just the basic view but also to modify it, rectify accuracies, and even delete the records. By guaranteeing you this level of access, SSI not only enhances personal agency but also ensures transparency, data accuracy, and trust.

- **Principle of transparency:** This principle provides the transparency in the identity mechanism. Every mechanism in the identity such as algorithms to verify or share the identity data must be transparent to the individuals. This is not about security but about entrusting individuals with their personal data such as where their personal data goes, how the data is verified, and the reason for requests or sharing. This clarity helps individuals make informed decisions about the data.

- **Principle of persistence:** The persistence of identity is important. In conventional identity systems, identities are subject to expiration or subject to sudden invalidation due to various reasons. An identity in SSI is conceived to be as persistent as one's physical existence, and the system is designed to remain consistent and undisturbed. By ensuring that an identity is long-lasting, individuals are safeguarded against disruption or losses. In SSI, identity also means that individuals have a stable and continuous footprint, ensuring that the history, credentials, and reputation can be consistently referenced with the identity data.

- **Principle of portability:** The principle at the core of SSI regarding seamless portability and universal recognition of identity credentials includes the concepts of interoperability, standardization, and mutual recognition. Legally, it necessitates an international consensus on the norms, standards, and protocols for identity verification, much like the way passports are universally accepted due to international treaties and agreements. This principle requires a legal framework that recognizes and enforces the validity of digital identities across different jurisdictions, ensuring that credentials are accepted and users can rely on them anywhere, akin to legal instruments. It also involves data protection and privacy laws, ensuring that as identity data is portable across borders, it adheres to stringent security standards, respecting individual privacy rights and minimizing data breaches. This legal interoperability not only enhances the user experience by facilitating smooth digital interactions but also upholds the integrity and trustworthiness of digital identities in a globally connected digital ecosystem.

- **Principle of interoperability:** The principle of interoperability in SSI systems emphasizes the need for a harmonized legal infrastructure that supports the recognition, collaboration, and validation of digital identities across various platforms and jurisdictions. It calls for the dissolution of isolated systems through the adoption of standardized protocols, data formats, and communication methods, much like the legal principles governing international trade or electronic transactions where different systems and nations agree on common standards for the exchange of goods and services and electronic data. Organizations such as W3C are instrumental in developing these standards, which, when legally endorsed and incorporated into national and international law, facilitate seamless, secure, and legally recognized exchange and validation of identity data across the SSI ecosystem. This approach encourages legal interoperability, reducing barriers and enhancing trust in digital transactions, while ensuring compliance with various jurisdictional regulations concerning privacy and data protection.

- **Principle of consent:** The core principle of explicit consent within the SSI ecosystem mandates that any interaction or transaction involving an individual's identity data must be explicitly authorized by the individual. This is akin to the legal doctrines of informed consent and contractual agreements, where the individual's autonomy and right to privacy are paramount. The SSI framework requires that consent must be an active, ongoing process, rather than a one-time or passive agreement, ensuring that individuals have continual control over their personal data. This is typically operationalized through the use of cryptographic proofs or digital signatures that provide a secure and verifiable means of granting permission. Legally, this principle is aligned with stringent data protection and privacy regulations, such as GDPR in the European Union, which emphasizes the right of individuals to control their personal data and obligations of entities to obtain clear, affirmative consent for data processing activities. By embedding explicit consent into the design of SSI systems, it ensures that the legal rights of individuals are respected and upheld in every transaction involving personal identity data.

- **Principle of protection:** This principle emphasizes the prioritization of an individual's data security and privacy, advocating for a minimalistic and need-to-know basis approach in personal data sharing. The principle encourages the use of technologies such as zero knowledge proofs or selective disclosure mechanisms, allowing individuals to prove certain attributes, such as age or eligibility, without revealing extraneous personal information. This method legally supports the individual's right to privacy and autonomy over personal data, while also adhering to the principles of necessity and least privilege, minimizing the amount of personal data collected and retained and thereby reducing the risk and impact of potential data breaches. It's a reflection of evolving legal standards that prioritize not just the security of data but also the discretion and rights of individuals in digital transactions.

- **Principle of minimization:** This principle is based on using the minimum amount of information when it comes to personal data. This principle has to be implemented for the data store by using cryptographic techniques such as zero-knowledge proofs. Sharing an age and not a full date of birth is an example of this principle; it helps with privacy and reduces the data liability for service providers because it reduces the amount of data compromised in cyberattacks and data breaches.

Benefits of SSI

SSI is a disruptive concept in digital identities and provides a multitude of advantages, fundamentally transforming the way digital identities are used.

- The first benefit is that SSI empowers you by giving you full control over the identity data, effectively shifting the centralized control to a decentralized control. That is, you have the autonomy to determine who can access the personal data and how it can be used.

- The second benefit is that SSI enables you to protect your privacy by allowing you to share only the specific data required for that particular interaction; that is, you share only what is needed. This granularity in sharing the data safeguards privacy and minimizes the risk of breaches, theft, etc.

- The third benefit is that SSI gives you full control over your data such as the ability to grant and revoke access to the identity data at any time. This fosters trust in digital interactions because you can respond dynamically to changing circumstances.

Challenges of SSI

As I mentioned, the SSI represents a disruption in digital identities and provides greater control, privacy, and security for you, but there are few challenges during SSI implementation and usage.

- SSI is a new concept, and currently the benefits are not widely known, especially in the general population around the world. This challenge will be crucial for acceptance. This requires big tech companies and organizations educating the public.

- Interoperability is a big challenge across different SSI platforms. Currently there is no universal SSI standard for interoperability, but the W3C is working on this. Still, it requires time and acceptance across tech communities.

- Regulation is complex. As you know, SSI is disruptive to the traditional identity management and regulatory framework, but still technology availability is minimal.

Addressing these challenges is crucial for realizing the full potential of SSI and redefining the way you interact with digital identities.

The Role of the Blockchain in Decentralized Identities

In this section, I'll introduce you to the blockchain and its capabilities. It is useful for you to understand the basics of blockchain technology in order to understand decentralization. Essentially, the blockchain is a decentralized and distributed ledger technology. It evolved primarily through the development of smart contracts and has significantly broadened its applications beyond simple peer-to-peer transactions, leading to an era of decentralized apps (DApps) and more robust solutions for fast and secure transactions. Initially, Bitcoin introduced Blockchain 1.0, which was primarily focused on creating a decentralized ledger for transactions. However, Ethereum leverages smart contracts to decentralize virtually any digital process, not just currency transactions. These contracts are self-executing agreements encoded on the blockchain, facilitating direct interactions between parties without the need for intermediaries and thus streamlining and automating various digital activities. It provides a secure, transparent, and tamper-proof foundation for digital transactions and data management. The blockchain operates by organizing data into a series of records that are interconnected in a chronological chain, and each block contains a cryptographic hash of the preceding block. This creates a strong and unbreakable link. This interlocking structure makes it extremely challenging to alter or erase data without detection by all participants on the network. This inherent transparency and security has helped the adoption rate of blockchain in different industries.

It is important to understand blockchain capabilities when deciding whether to use it for a particular application. Figure 5-1 shows the four major capabilities.

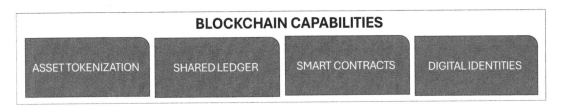

Figure 5-1. *Blockchain capabilities*

Asset Tokenization

Asset tokenization enables real-world tangible or intangible assets such as traditional currencies, works of art, commodities, or certificates of ownership through digital tokens securely recorded on a blockchain. These assets possess uniqueness, making them distinguishable from one another. Unlike digital data that can be easily copied, assets are not duplicable in the same way. These unique assets can be represented and tracked using digital tokens. Each digital token on the blockchain corresponds to a specific asset, creating a secure and immutable link between the digital representation and the real-world assets.

For digital identity, the individual attributes such as your name, date of birth, and biometric data are converted into digital tokens that are cryptographically secured and stored on a blockchain or decentralized identity platform. These tokens serve as verifiable proof of specific identity attributes or credentials issued by trusted entities such as government agencies, education, or financial institutions. You can own and control these digital identity tokens, and you can choose to share specific tokens with trusted parties.

Shared Ledger

The shared ledger or distributed ledger is a foundation of the blockchain. The shared ledger provides a solution to manage a transaction in a decentralized, secure, and tamper-resistant manner across a network of participants. This ledger eliminates a central authority and empowers a distributed network if participants can collectively maintain and validate the ledger's integrity. Each transaction recorded on the shared ledger is cryptographically linked to the previous ones, forming a chain of blocks that are sequentially connected. This makes it exceedingly challenging for any single user to alter the ledger's entry without consensus from the others.

For digital identities, the shared ledger offers a secure solution for managing and verifying personal information and credentials. This shared ledger provides a decentralized and tamper-resistant infrastructure to store the details. This means users are no longer bound by centralized authorities or intermediaries, because they can securely store and manage identity attributes in the ledger.

Smart Contracts

Smart contracts are autonomous, self-executing agreements and serve digital contracts with predefined rules and conditions. When the rules and conditions are met, they trigger automatic and tamper-resistance action. These contracts operate without any central or intermediaries, and they are immutable, transparent, and secure.

For digital identities, smart contracts help individuals interact with their digital identities, enhance verification process, and safeguard sensitive information. The smart contracts automate the identity verification processes by doing cross verification with government-issued IDs with trusted sources. Once verified, the contract can grant access to specific resources or services.

Digital Identities

A digital identity in the blockchain represents how individuals assert control over their personal information. The decentralized digital identities enable individuals to access digital services and experiences without relying on centralized authorities such as Google or Meta or Apple for authentication and identity verification. By eliminating the reliance on central authorities or third-party intermediaries, individuals limit the exposure of personal information.

The blockchain is a vast and intricate field with numerous aspects to explore, including the concept of blocks, chains, nodes, consensus algorithms, and various applications. For those interested in delving deeper into the subject, there are many excellent books, online courses, and other resources to help you gain a comprehensive understanding of blockchain technology.

The Role of Smart Contracts in Digital Identity

As I mentioned, smart contracts are self-executing, tamper-proof contracts with predefined rules and conditions written in code. They operate on blockchain technology, ensuring trust, transparency, and immutability. Smart contracts enable automated and secure execution of various processes without relying on intermediaries.

Smart contracts are instrumental in achieving the core principles of SSI. They play a pivotal role in transforming the way an identity is managed and utilized, and they help in disclosure, data ownership, and identity verification.

The smart contract enables the disclosure of selective information and allows you to share only specific identity attributes to the requesting parties. If you want to complete the know-your-customer (KYC) verification, you can use a smart contract to confirm the identity without revealing other details.

Smart contracts help you to control your digital identity information and enable you to store your identity data in the blockchain. You can grant or revoke access to your information at any time through the execution of smart contracts, reducing the risk of data breaches and unauthorized use.

In the identity verification process, the smart contract provides a trustless (a fundamental quality of decentralized blockchain and crypto) mechanism for verifying identities. For a service provider such as an e-commerce application or delivery app, smart contracts can be used to confirm the validity of identity claims without disclosing sensitive information. This ensures that the verification process is secure and efficient and doesn't require you to divulge more information than necessary. For example, in an e-commerce application, the app can verify your identity without needing to know your full name or other sensitive information.

Present-Day Identity and DIDs

Currently we use a centralized identity to gain access to our accounts. Our email addresses and social network IDs are central access points for a wide array of online activities. However, this extended use has led to potential vulnerabilities. The providers of these IDs have the authority to revoke access at any time and misuse our data for any purpose. This centralized control puts you at risk of losing access to your own data and online presence and most importantly its privacy.

In contrast, the DIDs represent a shift in the way you use and manage digital identities. The DIDs are not tied to any central authority, providing a level of independence and autonomy. This means that access to one's DID is solely in the hands of the user. The unique characteristics of DIDs, such as immutability, censorship resistance, and tamper evasiveness, are critical to any identity system aiming to provide self-ownership. This distinction underlines the significant advantages of DIDs over present-day identity methods.

Table 5-1 summarizes the key differences between present-day identity and DIDs.

Table 5-1. *Present-Day Identities vs. DIDs*

Characteristics	Present-Day Identities	DIDs
Ownership	Owned by a third party (for example, Google, Facebook, Apple)	User-owned
Control	Controlled by third party	User controlled
Immutability	Low	High
Censorship Resistance	Low	High
Tamper Evasiveness	Low	High
Privacy	Low	High

DID Types

There are two types of DIDs you can create.

- Public DID
- Pairwise DID

Public DID

Public DIDs are identifiers that you consciously link with data intended for public access. This data can include information such as a brief biography, a photograph, or other details that you are comfortable sharing publicly. These IDs are suitable when you intend for an activity or interaction to be linked to your identity in a way that can be verified by others such as public online services. The advantages of public DIDs are verifiability, trust and reputation, and portability. Use a public DID when you want to be easily verifiable by others or to build trust and reputation, such as in professional or public-facing areas.

Pairwise DID

Pairwise DIDs are generated whenever you want to isolate your interactions and prevent correlation, which means you are enhancing privacy and security by creating a new DID for each interaction or relationship. Each interaction of relationship is associated with a unique DID. This means that even if someone were to obtain one of your pairwise DIDs, they wouldn't be able to trace your other interactions; it enhances the privacy. This type of DID is useful when your top priority is privacy. This help you to have a higher degree of anonymity and control over online services. The advantages of pairwise DID are privacy protection, control over personal information, and enhanced security.

Use pairwise DIDs when you want to have full privacy and want to prevent the correlation of your online activities, granularized control of your information, such as who can access your details, and when you want more security identity interaction for each services.

How Does Decentralization Work?[1]

Digital identity incorporates technologies and standards to provide essential identity attributes such as self-ownership and censorship resistance that arise from the limitations of the existing identity management system. Defining a decentralized identity management system comprises the following components, as shown in Figure 5-2:

- W3C decentralized identifiers
- Decentralized system (blockchain and ledgers)
- DID user agents
- DIF universal resolver
- DIF identity hubs
- DID attestation
- Decentralized apps and services

---

[1] https://www.microsoft.com/en-us/security/business/solutions/decentralized-identity

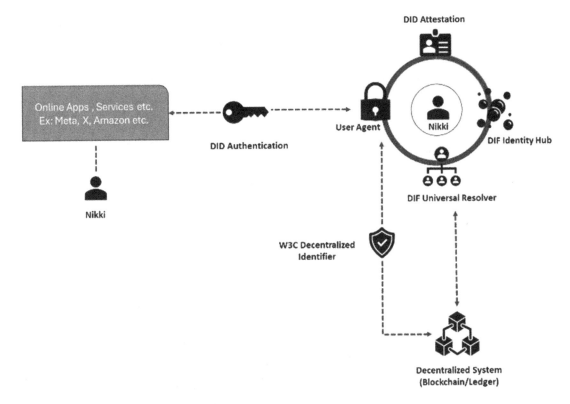

Figure 5-2. *Decentralized identifier*

W3C Decentralized Identifiers[2]

DIDs are defined by the World Wide Web Consortium (W3C) and are designed as an independent central authority allowing you to have control over your own digital identities. These digital identities are globally unique and associated with metadata in the form of a JSON document, which contain confidential information such as public keys, authentication details, and service endpoints. The DIDs are not controlled by any centralized authority; instead, they are controlled by you or your organization.

A DID is a unique, persistent identifier that does not require a centralized registration authority because it is fully under the control of the DID subject, and it's verifiable. It is a simple string made up of three parts, as shown in Figure 5-3.

---

[2] https://www.w3.org/TR/did-core/

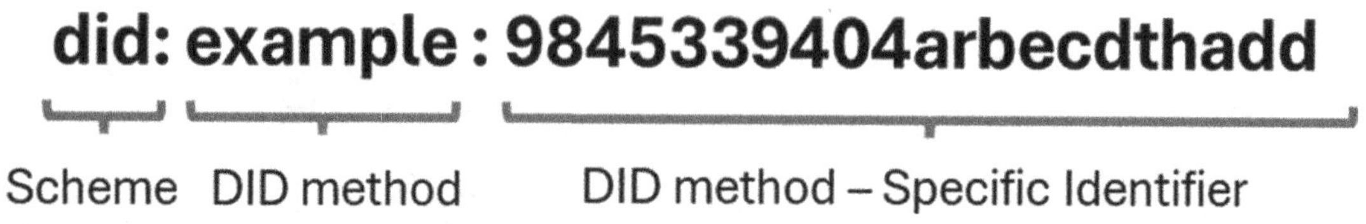

did: example : 9845339404arbecdthadd

Scheme   DID method   DID method – Specific Identifier

Figure 5-3. *DID identifier*

These are the three parts:

- **DID scheme identifier:** The scheme is always the string "did" and signifies that the URI is a DID according to that specific scheme. It's a static part of the identifier that indicates the text string is a decentralized identifier.

- **DID method:** The DID method is a specific mechanism defined in a DID method specification, which includes a set of operations (create, read, update, deactivate) and the method-specific namespace. For example, "btcr" might refer to a method using Bitcoin's blockchain, and "ethr" could refer to Ethereum. Each DID method is typically associated with a specific type of verifiable data registry, such as a blockchain or a distributed ledger, and provides detailed instructions for how DIDs and DID documents can be created, resolved, updated, and deactivated within the particular system.

- **DID method-specific identifier:** This is a unique set of characters generated by the DID method that is used to create a unique identifier for the DID subject within the method's namespace. This portion of the DID is what distinguishes one DID from another within the same method.

A sample DID document is shown here:

```
{
"@context": [
        "https://www.w3.org/ns/did/v1",
        "https://w3id.org/security/suites/ed25519-2020/v1"
            ]
        "id" : "did:example:9845339404arbecdthadd",
```

```
    "authentication": [{
    "id": did:example: 9845339404arbecdthadd#keys-1",
    "type": ED25519VerificationKey2020",
    "controller": "did:example: 9845339404arbecdthadd",
    "publickeyMultibase": "sdsuzfhehlsflhdfdsreywerewcdhjeerewr"
    }]
}
```

Decentralized System (Blockchain and Ledgers)

Decentralized systems such as the blockchain and ledgers are essential for the implementation of DIDs. DIDs are rooted in decentralized systems because these technologies provide the mechanisms and features required for a decentralized public key infrastructure (DPKI). DPKI is a cryptographic system that allows you to verify the identity of other users without the need of a trusted third party. This can be accomplished by using public key cryptography, which allows you to create and share public and private keys. Public keys are used to verify the authenticity of messages signed with the corresponding private keys.

Blockchain and ledgers store data and DPKI metadata securely. Once information is recorded, it becomes virtually immutable. This characteristic is important for safeguarding DPKI metadata. This level of security provides confidence and trust in the integrity of digital identities. With the appropriate permissions, anyone can access and scrutinize the information stored within this system. This openness is instrumental in engendering trust, as it empowers any interested party to independently verify the authenticity of the DID document. This accessibility not only contributes to transparency but also decentralizes the process of identity verification.

DID User Agents

DID user agents are essential tools in the realm of DIDs, acting as intermediaries that empower individuals to manage and control their DIDs. Similar to a digital Swiss Army knife, these agents facilitate various functionalities related to decentralized identity management. They enable users to create new DIDs, manage their different personas or roles, control which information is shared and with whom, and even revoke or update permission as needed. These agents also provide a user-friendly interface for interacting with the complex, underlying technologies of DIDs and the blockchain. By handling the cryptographic keys and other technical details, DID user agents ensure that even those without deep technical knowledge can maintain control over their digital identities, making the process of verifying, sharing, and protecting personal data smoother and more initiative. The functionalities are as follows:

- **Creating your unique DID:** With a DID user agent, the process is designed to be user-friendly and secure, guiding you step-by-step. It begins by choosing a DID method appropriate for your needs, which dictates how your identifier will be created, resolved, and interacted with on a specific blockchain or network. The user agent then assists in generating a unique cryptographic key pair, ensuring that your DID is secure and tamper-evident. This key pair is used to create your DID, which is then recorded on the respective decentralized system, such as a blockchain, making it verifiable and tamper-resistant.

- **Managing your data and permissions:** With the DID user agent, managing your data and permissions becomes a streamlined and user-centric experience. After creating your DID, it is associated with a DID document, which is a JSON file that contains information about the DID, including public keys, authentication protocols, and service endpoints, as shown in the previous code snippet. This document is where you store various pieces of data related to your identity and specify how and by whom this data will be accessed. The user agent provides a user interface for adding, updating, or removing information from your DID document. It also allows you to set specific permissions for different entities, defining who can view or verify certain pieces of information. For example, you might allow a healthcare provider to verify your age but not your home address. This granular control extends to consent management, enabling you to grant or revoke access to your data as circumstances change.

- **Validating claims linked to your DID:** DIDs serve as more than static identifiers; they are dynamic, capable of holding various claims or assertions made about the DID subject. (The DID subject can be a person, group, or organization, and can be physical or digital). These claims might include assertions about personal attributes, qualifications, or affiliation, such as educational degrees or professional licenses. The role of a DID user agent in this context is to help validate and manage these claims. It does so by interfacing with trusted entities that issue these claims, known as *verifiable credentials.* The user agent can verify the cryptographic proofs attached to these credentials, ensuring they were indeed issued by the claimed authority and have not been tampered with. It checks the validity, authenticity, and revocation status of claims, presenting a reliable and updated status to you and those you consent to share this information with. By facilitating the verification process, the user agent ensures that the dynamic data linked to your DID is trustworthy, thereby protecting you from potential misinformation claims.

- **Precise control over your digital information:** With a DID user agent, you can exert precise and granular control over your digital information, making a significant shift in how personal data is managed and shared. This control is exercised through robust permission settings and consent mechanisms embedded within the user agent's interface. As a user, you can specify exactly who is allowed to access your data, delineate the scope of what they can see or use, and set the time limits on this access. For example, you might allow a financial institution to verify your identity for a loan application but restrict access after the process is complete. This selective sharing reduces the risk of data breaches and unauthorized use, as each piece of data is accessible only to vetted parties and for only as long as needed. The user agent extends functionality to revoke, grant, or update permissions in real time.

- **Streamlining interactions and services:** DID user agents significantly streamline digital interactions and services by offering a more efficient and privacy-preserving alternative to the traditional methods of identity verification. Instead of repeatedly filling out forms or submitting the same piece of information for different services, you can present your verified DIDs and associated claims. These DIDs, backed by verifiable credentials from any government agencies or universities or reputed organizations, act as digital passports, granting access to various services and platforms with minimum hassle. As a result, you can navigate the digital realm more fluidly, accessing services quickly and securely.

- **Regulated and legal landscape:** The user agents adhere to the modern regulations, data privacy, and user rights. By facilitating the management of DIDs, these user agents enable users to share only the necessary data, providing explicit consent each time their information is accessed or used. The user agents support the right to data portability and the right to be forgotten, both crucial aspects of regulatory frameworks such as GDPR.

There are various applications available as a user agent, such as Microsoft Entra Verified Id, VIDChain, IdRamp, ONTO, Hyperledger Indy, SelfKey, and C2Identity.

DIF Universal Resolver

The DIF universal resolver is a server that provides a standard means of looking up and resolving DIDs across decentralized systems by using the collection of DID drivers to resolve DIDs on a specific blockchain or decentralized system.

When you query the DIF universal resolver for a DID, the resolver will first check to see if it has a DID driver for the blockchain that the DID is registered on. If it is found, the resolver will use the DID driver to resolve the DID and return the DID document that encapsulates the DPKI metadata associated with the DID and return an error message if it did not find the DID driver in a blockchain.

The DID resolution/universal resolution is the process by which a DID document is retrieved for a specific DID, essentially "reading" the DID. This is one of the four fundamental operations defined for DIDs, along with create, update, and deactivate. The process and details of these operations vary based on the specific DID method used, as each method may have its unique protocol for interacting with the underlying verifiable data registry, as shown in Figure 5-4. The software and hardware capable of executing these processes is known as the *DID resolver*.

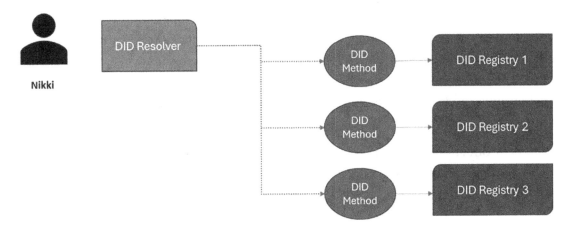

Figure 5-4. *The DID resolver supports multiple DID methods*

DIF Identity Hubs

DID identity hubs are a pivotal component in the DID ecosystem, providing a secure, off-chain solution for personal data storage, distinct from public ledgers. While public ledgers are excellent for distributing identifiers and public keys, they are not suitable for storing sensitive personal data due to their immutable and sometimes public nature. Identity hubs address these concerns by offering a decentralized personal data store that grants users complete control and autonomy over their information. These hubs allow individuals to securely store sensitive data such as profile information, official documents, and contact details. Crucially, they enable users to share this information selectively, granting access only to the required data and keeping a record of who has access. This ensures that the data usage occurs solely with the user's explicit consent.

APIs to Access the Identity Hub

The standardization of the interface for data storage and retrieval in identity hubs represents a significant advancement in user autonomy and flexibility within the decentralized identity space. A standard interface means that users are not bound to a single provider or platform for their identity hub; instead, they have the freedom to choose where to host their hub. The choice is critical for ensuring data portability and avoiding vendor lock-in. Users can seamlessly transfer their data between different hubs if they decide to switch providers, maintaining continuous control over their personal information. Additionally, this standardization facilitates interoperability between different services and applications, as each identity hub, regardless of the provider, adheres to the same set of protocols for data access and management.

The API offers various interfaces, each designed for specific functionalities, to facilitate efficient data management and control in decentralized identity system. The interfaces are as follows:

- **Collections:** Collections serve as the central repository for personal data storage. This interface uses user-related data including documents, profile details, and other personal data for storing and management.

- **Profile:** A profile contains metadata related to a user's DID, such as DID type (individual, business, etc.), names, and contact information. This helps in categorizing and retrieving identity-related data efficiently.

- **Permissions:** This interface plays a vital role in maintaining data security and privacy. It manages access records, allowing users to grant, review, and revoke access to their data stored in other interfaces.

When developing an application that interacts with identity hubs, it's crucial to select the appropriate interface based on the specific requirements of the scenario. In most cases, the developers will primarily interact with the Collection interface for general data storage and retrieval.

Hub Data Model

Unlike traditional data storage systems that typically operate on a fixed schema dictating the type and structure of data to be stored, identity hubs employ a more flexible, semantic data model. In this model, each piece of data is self-descriptive, containing all the necessary metadata for interaction. This means the data stored in an identity hub is not constrained by predefined fields or formats; instead, it can dynamically include information about its own nature and purpose. This metadata might encompass attributes such as the data type, permissions, and context-specific details, allowing for more nuanced and intelligent handling of data.

The semantic model enhances interoperability, as it enables different systems or applications to understand and process the data without needing prior knowledge of a specific schema. This flexibility is crucial in decentralized environments where data comes from diverse sources and needs to be understood and utilized by various entities. It allows identity hubs to adapt to a wide range of user data requirements and scenarios, ensuring that users can store and manage their personal information in a way that is both versatile and user centric.

Commits

In an identity hub, data is structured and managed in a unique way, as described earlier, using a concept akin to version control systems such as Git or other source control systems. Each row of data is referred to as an *object*, and modifications to these objects are recorded as *commits*. Each commit represents a change to an object, similar to how a Git commit reflects a change in a file or set of files. When data is added or modified in an identity hub, a new commit is created and sent to the hub. Conversely, to retrieve the latest state of an object, the system fetches and sequentially applies all the commits associated with that object. This approach offers several advantages.

- First, it supports the replication protocol of the hub, allowing multiple instances of the hub to synchronize data effectively. This is crucial for maintaining consistency across different user devices or access points.

- Second, the commit-based structure creates a traceable and auditable history of changes for each object. When commits are signed with DID, it adds a layer of security and accountability, as each change can be attributed to a specific entity.

- Lastly, this model is advantageous for scenarios requiring offline data modifications and subsequent conflict resolution upon reconnection, as the history of changes is clearly delineated and can be systematically reconciled. This design not only enhances the robustness of reliability of data management in identity hubs but also aligns with the decentralized and user-centric principles of SSI systems.

Permissions

In identity hubs, the management of data access is governed by the Permission interface, utilizing specific entities known as Permission Grant objects. Central to this system is the principle that the DID, which owns the identity hub, retains full and unmitigated access rights. This means the owner of the DID can read, modify, write, and delete any data within a hub. To extend access to others, the owner creates Permissions Grant objects, each tailored to grant specific access rights to other DIDs. These objects define the scope and limitations of access, including which data can be accessed, the level of interaction permitted such as read-only or write access, and the duration for which the access is granted. This mechanism ensures a secure and controlled environment where data access is not only customizable but also clearly auditable.

Replication

The concept of identity hubs is based on the distributed architecture principle approach to data management, wherein a single DID can be associated with multiple hub instances. These instances, whether located in the cloud or edge devices or any other compatible infrastructure, are designed to replicate data among each other. This replication ensures that the user's personal data is not confined to a single location or provider but is instead distributed across various physical data stores.

Such a system offers significant advantages in terms of reliability, security, and user autonomy. Users are not dependent on a single cloud provider or centralized storage, mitigating the risks associated with data availability and single points of failure. By enabling the operation of identity hubs on personal devices, users gain physical ownership and control over their data copies, enhancing security and privacy.

Encryption

Identity hub encryption plays a crucial role in ensuring data protection by encrypting all data at the edge before being transmitted to any hub instances. This approach guarantees that hub providers never access the contents of an object in its unencrypted form, thus significantly enhancing data privacy and security.

DID Attestation

DID attestation refers to assertions or statements that are signed by a decentralized identifier following established formats and protocols. These attestations perform a fundamental role in identity system and empower you to create and present validity claims about identity. These attestations are typically used to verify the identity of individuals or organizations and can be used to verify a wide range of claims such as name, age, address, citizenship, education, employment, health, criminal history, etc. These attestations are cryptographically signed, which means they can be trusted to be authentic and tamper-proof.

Decentralized Apps and Services

Decentralized apps (DApps) represent a significant shift from traditional, centralized applications, as they are built on decentralized networks, primarily blockchain technology. The core component of a DApp includes a smart contract, which serves as the backend logic and is deployed on the blockchain, and a back-end application and user interface, as shown in Figure 5-5. DApps operate on a consensus mechanism, where changes to the application are made based on the agreement of the majority of its users, fostering transparency and collective governance.

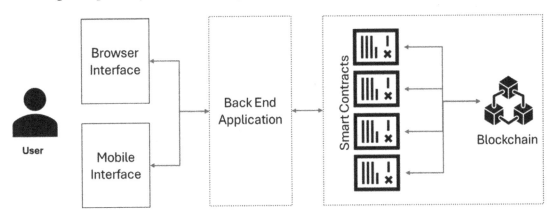

Figure 5-5. *Decentralized application*

The DIDs and identity hubs together can create a foundation for a new type of DApp with various features and capabilities and a wide variety of uses such as provider-agnostic serverless apps; semantic, model-less storage of data objects; and an open data layer.

Serverless Applications

The DIDs and identity hub foundation are designed to provide a provider-agnostic serverless app that can be written as a client-side package that stores your data in the identity hub regardless of where the identity hub instances are located. These apps can interact with any user's identity hub through a standard set of APIs.

Semantic and Model-less Storage

DID systems enable the semantic and model-less storage of data objects. These data objects can come from various shared schemes or datasets used by apps, services, and organizations for collaborations and data exchanges. This design allows for flexible and efficient storage of data without being tied to rigid data models.

Examples of DApps are decentralized social media platforms, decentralized marketplaces, decentralized ride-sharing apps, decentralized food delivery apps, and decentralized travel apps.

Decentralized Social Media Platforms

A decentralized social media platform represents a significant shift in how you engage with social networking online. In this design, you are empowered to store your profile data and posts within your identity hubs. This design change puts you firmly in control of your data, allowing you to dictate who has access to the personal information. On a present-day social media platform where your data is locked into a single provider's ecosystem, this decentralized model ensures data portability and flexibility. With this design, you have the freedom to choose the social media platform you prefer while maintaining ownership of your identity.

This design enhances your privacy and also fosters a more open and interconnected digital landscape, where you can seamlessly interact across various platforms while retaining complete authority over your data.

Decentralized Ride-Sharing Apps

This type of app provides a transformative paradigm to the world of transportation services. In this design, you have the ability to share your real-time location and availability through your identity hubs. This innovative design shift eliminates the necessity for a centralized intermediary like with present-day sharing companies.

Instead, drivers and passengers can directly connect and coordinate rides with each other. For example, if you are looking for a ride, you can easily discover nearby drivers who are available; meanwhile, drivers can find passengers in their vicinity with the decentralized network. By removing the aggregators, a decentralized ride-sharing app offers a more efficient, cost-effective, and use-centric transportation solution, fostering a peer-to-peer economy.

This type of decentralized app could revolutionize the entire industry, which would need to redesign their aggregator apps to suit decentralization.

Real-World DID Scenario

In the scenario shown in Figure 5-6, Nikki can use a DID to request a digital copy of her health insurance card, issued by her insurance company against her DID. She can choose to present her insurance ID to any hospital, which can independently verify the issuance of health insurance and status.

Here is the step-by-step approach:

- Nikki requests a digital copy of her insurance card from her insurance company.

- Nikki provides her digital insurance to a hospital.

- The hospital verifies the insurance using a DID resolver. The DID resolver validates the issuer of the insurance, as well as the time, date, covering amount of issuance, and status.

- If the insurance is valid, the potential hospital can be confident that Nikki has insurance from the insurance company and her insurance is valid for coverage.

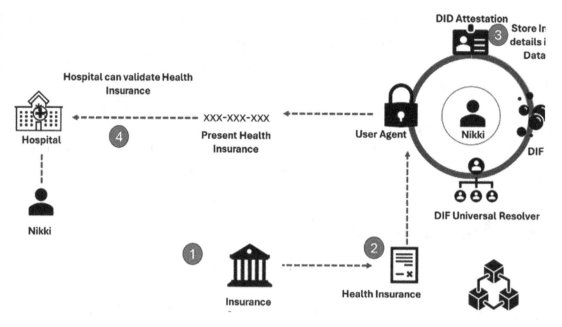

Figure 5-6. *DID scenario to verify health insurance*

The process of sharing digital insurance through a DID offers several distinct advantages over the traditional practices of providing a physical insurance card and manually verifying the coverage status. For example, it provides enhanced security as the insurance is fortified by cryptographic signatures directly from the insurance company. With a digital insurance tied to Nikki's DID, she gains the ability to effortlessly share it with anyone across the coverage countries. This removes the geographical boundaries and enables instant, seamless validation of insurance.

Acquiring a DID

To obtain a DID, you need to follow a few steps. First, you need to download a DID user agent. This type of application is designed to assist you in managing various aspects of your DID.

With present-day identity management, your identity data is stored in a central database, such as a government database or with social media tech companies. In a decentralized system, your identity data is stored in your DID user agent app. The key difference is that with a decentralized identity, you have complete control over your own identity data. Just like you associate the DID user agent with your present-day web browser and the web browser manages various aspects of your Internet access, the DID user agent manages your decentralized identifier in the following ways:

- **Identifier creation:** The user agent app helps you to create your unique DIDs.

- **Authentication:** It assists in the authentication processes related to your DIDs, ensuring that you can prove your ownership or control over them.

- **Data encryption:** It encrypts your data associated with your identity and ensures the privacy of your identity-related information.

- **Management of keys and permissions:** This app helps you to manage cryptographic keys and permissions associated with your DIDs. This is crucial for controlling access and interactions related to your identity.

This application is a single point for you to manage your DIDs, as shown in Figure 5-7.

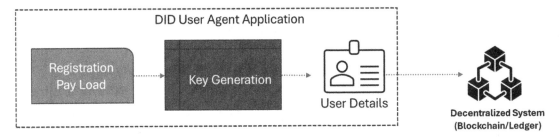

Figure 5-7. *DID user agent registration process*

Here's a breakdown of the steps. First, the DID user agent application collects and assembles user registration payload. This payload includes the following:

- References to cryptographic key associated with the DID

- Information about identity hub services that may be used for various identity-related functions

- Public data or values needed for recovery purposes, such as account recovery

The second step is generating a device key. This key is used to secure the user's interactions and data within the DID system and creates an encrypted owner recovery bundle. This bundle contains sensitive information that you may require to recover your identity in the case of loss or compromise.

The third step is to push the assembled DID registration payload to the decentralized system. The choice of decentralized system and the specific protocol used for this registration depends on your selections and capabilities of the DID implementation you have chosen.

The actual DID information is stored off-chain, which means it is stored separately from the chain, but this off-chain data remains under your control.

DID Discovery or Lookup

Once you have created a DID by using the DID user agent application, you can use this DID to authenticate yourself and manage your digital identity. You can also interact with other DIDs or search for another DID. This could be useful when you want to interact with someone or some services that use DIDs.

As I mentioned, the DID user agent application is used for managing DIDs and related identity tasks. In the context of looking up other DIDs, the user agent application can communicate with external services, i.e., the DIF universal resolver, to facilitate the process. The DIF universal resolver can resolve DIDs across DID implementations by using an appropriate driver or interface with the decentralized system that DID is rooted in and retrieve corresponding DID document, which contains critical details about DID, such as public keys, service endpoints, and other metadata. The ability to discover different DIDs within a decentralized system may vary depending on the specific DID implementation.

DID Authentication with Other Services

There are several ways you can use your DID to interact with other services, but the most important interaction is DID authentication. This process allows you to prove your identity to external services. To authenticate, you need to disclose the unique identifier associated with your DID to the other service. The other services that you are interacting with wants to verify your DID authenticity. The services look up or discover your DID through a DIF universal resolver. As mentioned, this resolver retrieves the associated

DPKI metadata. Upon retrieving the DPKI metadata, the other service applications generate a challenge to verify you. This challenges utilizes the public key references that is present in the metadata. The other service application initiates a handshake with you by using the challenge-response mechanism; you need to respond to this challenge to complete the authentication. If you are able to successfully complete this challenge handshake, it demonstrates that you are the rightful owner of the DID. This way, you prove the authenticity of your unique identification.

Let's consider an example. Say Nikki wants to authenticate her DID in a social media application, as shown in Figure 5-8. First, Nikki will share her unique identity of her DID to social media application. Second, the social media application looks up or discovers her unique identity by using a DIF universal resolver. Third, the universal resolver looks up Nikki's DID document by using a driver and sends back this document to the social media app.

Figure 5-8. *DID authentication process*

Fourth, the social media app extracts the public key and sends a challenge to Nikki to check the authenticity. Fifth, Nikki completes this challenge by using her private key. Finally, the social media platform authenticates Nikki.

DID Data Stores and Sharing Process

Currently, we are storing data either in our personal devices or with third-party storage such as Google Drive, Dropbox, iCloud, and OneDrive. These are typically generic storages not designed for secure identity interactions.

A DID uses the Decentralized Identity Foundation (DIF) identity hubs to store the personal data, taking a different approach than present-day storage. This hub is user-controlled and off-chain, providing you with greater control over your data. The data is shared through a DIF user agent. You have the authority to determine who you share your data with and the level of granularity of such sharing. The user agent app requests the DIF identity hub to verify the DPKI metadata with service endpoints associated with the DID. This means that the metadata associated with a DID makes the direct request to the appropriate identity hub.

The data in the identity hub is edge-encrypted. This means it is encrypted on your end before being stored and applies your access control policies to the data, ensuring that the data access controlled by you. This approach ensures privacy.

The identity hub serves as the facilitator in a decentralized system, and its primary function is to store and manage your data and facilitate the secure exchange of messages within the identity system. In terms of limiting access to your data, the identity hubs do not possess the keys necessary to decrypt your data stored in the hub. This means that the hosts cannot access the actual content of your data. You have full control over your data and can revoke or remove your encrypted data from any service or entity at any point of time. This grants you sovereignty over your data.

Permission for accessing and interacting with your data is signed with your decentralized identifier keys, and data stored in the hub is encrypted in accordance with these permissions, ensuring that only the authorized entity can access and decrypt the data.

Data Instances and Replication

The identity hub's key characteristic is that it can replicate across multiple instances and infrastructure boundaries. This helps you to store your data with any provider or create your own identity hub. These instances can synchronize and replicate data to ensure that there is a shared and consistent state of your identity data across various identity hub providers. This whole design makes identity hubs more resilient to failure, because if one instance of an identity hub goes down, the data can still be accessed from other instances.

Cryptography

Cryptography is a method of protecting information by transforming it into a secure format that is unreadable to anyone except those who possess the key to decipher it. The word *cryptography* comes from the Greek words *crypt*, which means hidden, and *graphy*, means writing. The cryptography concept uses mathematical theories and complex algorithms to encrypt and decrypt data, ensuring that only intended recipients can understand and process the information, thereby preventing unauthorized access.

These algorithms play a crucial role in DIDs. The fundamental cryptography is used to generate keys, which are essential for securing digital communications, digital signing, and verification.

Modern cryptography encompasses sophisticated algorithms and ciphers, crucial for encrypting and decrypting data to safeguard it against unauthorized access. Techniques such as 128-bit and 256-bit encryption keys are commonly used. Currently, one of the most prominent ciphers is the Advanced Encryption Standard (AES).

Cryptography Features

Cryptography has the following features, and each feature plays a crucial role in securing digital communication and data, ensuring that they remain private, unaltered, attributable, and accessible only to authorized parties. Together these features form a backbone of trust and security in the digital world, enabling safe and confidential information exchange across various platforms. These cryptography features are as follows:

- **Confidentiality:** This ensures that information is accessible only to those who are meant to see it. For DIDs, this means the digital information, whether it is in transit or at rest in blockchain storage, can be decrypted and understood only by the owner of it. This feature is crucial for protecting sensitive information from unauthorized access.

- **Integrity:** This feature guarantees that the information remains unaltered during storage or transmission. Integrity checks are vital to ensure that data has not been tampered with or modified in any way. This is important in the DID ecosystem. It allows the receiver to verify that the received information is exactly what the sender intended to send, without any unauthorized alterations. If any change is made to the data, either intentionally or accidentally, it can be detected by the recipient.

- **Nonrepudiation:** This prevents the sender of the information from later denying the transmission or the creation of the sent information. This can be achieved through digital signatures and other forms of digital verification, providing proof of the origin and authenticity of the data.

- **Authentication:** Authentication in cryptography involves confirming the identities of the parties involved in the communication. It ensures that the sender is indeed who they claim to be and that the information is being sent and received by the intended parties. This feature is essential to preventing unauthorized access.

Types of Cryptography

Many types of cryptographic algorithms are available, and they vary in complexity, security, and usage.

- **Symmetric key cryptography:** This encryption system uses a single, shared key for both the encryption and decryption of messages. Both the sender and the receiver use this common key, making the process straightforward and efficient. Symmetric key systems are known for their speed and simplicity. However, they pose a challenge in key distribution: the key must be shared between the sender and the receiver in a secure manner to maintain confidentiality. Popular symmetric keys are Data Encryption System (DES) and Advanced Encryption System (AES).

- **Hash functions:** Hash functions do not involve the use of keys; instead, they compute a fixed-length hash value based on the plaintext input. This hash value acts as a unique identifier for the given input. The critical aspect of hash functions is that they are one-way. It's virtually impossible to reverse-engineer the original plaintext from the hash value. This feature makes hash functions ideal for securing sensitive data such as passwords.

- **Asymmetric key cryptography:** This method uses a pair of keys: a public key and a private key for encryption and decryption, respectively. The public key, as the name suggests, is openly shared and used to encrypt information. The private key, kept confidential by the receiver, is used for decryption. The strength of this system lies in the fact that even if the public key is known to everyone, only the intended receiver, who possesses the private key, can decrypt the message. The RSA algorithm is the most popular asymmetric key cryptography.

Cryptography in DIDs

Cryptography serves as the backbone of DID systems, ensuring their security, integrity, and privacy. Cryptography offers a secure trustworthy framework for managing digital identities. Through the public key infrastructure (asymmetric keys) and digital signatures, the DID system provides a secure, private, and efficient means of handling identity data.

- **Public key infrastructure:** In the realm of DIDs, PKI plays a crucial role in creating and managing digital keys that enable secure communication and authentication. In this system, a pair of keys (public and private) is used. The key management facilitates the secure interaction between different entities in the decentralized identity ecosystem, ensuring that communications and transactions are both secure and authentic.

- **Digital signatures:** These are fundamental to establishing trust in a DID system. Verifiable credentials, such as digital IDs or certificates, are signed using digital signatures. This cryptographic technique ensures the authenticity of the credentials and prevents tampering. When a credential is digitally signed, it is cryptographically linked to the issuer (such as university certificates), making it possible to verify its origin and integrity without needing to contact the issuer directly.

- **Hash functions:** These are widely used in DID systems. They involve converting data into a fixed-size string of characters, which acts as a unique digital fingerprint of the data. This hash is generated in such a way that it's practically impossible to reverse engineer the original data from it. Hash functions are used to securely store and verify identity data. With sensitive information, only the hash of the data is kept, which ensures the privacy and security of the actual information. When verification is needed, the same hash function is applied to the presented data, and the result is compared with the stored hash. This method provides a secure way to verify information without exposing or directly handling sensitive data.

Establishing Credibility Between DIDs

Once DIDs are more established, anyone will be able to get one. But how will you be sure that a DID-based identity is legitimate? In this evolving ecosystem, DIDs have sought to gain legitimacy and trust through a process of endorsement. This process requires existing trust providers, which could be organizations, businesses, educational institutions, or government entities, to vouch for the authenticity of a DID-based identity. To substantiate the legitimacy, the DID has the power to create an attestation, such as a digital stamp of approval that includes independent verification of who issued the endorsement and when it was issued. These attestations are tangible evidence of a DID's credibility. By accumulating these attestations from multiple trust systems over time, the more endorsement and attestation you gathered, the more the credibility of your DID grows.

Present-day identity systems predominantly use email and account-based identities, whereas DIDs are not reliant on a central system to vouch for their legitimacy. Instead, DIDs are tied to cryptographic keys, providing a robust foundation for security and trust, and the DIDs are rooted in decentralized systems that maintain a shared, global lineage of operations related to DPKI. This global lineage serves as a trustworthy anchor, endorsing the reliability of DIDs.

In addition, a DID allows attestation by another trusted DIDs and independently verifiable claims signed by one or more DIDs. These claims make assertions about another DID's authenticity and attributes.

In the context of data integrity, DIDs use the blockchain and ledgers. These allow the secure logging of the time state of the data. This helps the data to be independently validated without having to trust another entity or organization.

Through all these endorsements, attestation, and the use of a decentralized system, DIDs have brought trust and authenticity to your digital identity.

Interoperability and Standards

The Decentralized Identity Foundation (DIF) is playing a central role in the development, discussion, and management of activities related to creating and sustaining an interoperable and open ecosystem for the decentralized identity stack.

The DIF possesses the capability to establish working groups with intellectual property rights (IPR) protection, produce specifications and standards, and provide infrastructure to support the broader decentralized identity community.

The following are a few available specifications in the DIF ecosystem.

DIDComm 2.0

DIDComm 2.0 enables secure communication between DIDs. It provides a standardized framework for secure messaging and data exchange in the decentralized identity space. This protocol supports multiple authentication methods such as SAML and OIDC and multiple encryption algorithms with message routing and discovery features. This protocol allows for a wide range of interactions, from simple request-response exchange to complex, multiparty scenarios. You can find more details about this protocol at `https://identity.foundation/didcomm-messaging/spec/v2.0`.

Well Known DID Configuration

The Well Known DID Configuration specification defines a standardized location where applications and services can discover essential information about a DI, such as its associated endpoints and supported protocols. This configuration simplifies the integration of DIDs into various applications and services in a bidirectional relationship through the use of cryptographically verifiable signatures that are associated with the DID's key materials. The DID configuration simplifies the process of discovering associated DIDs for a specific web origin. If you have the origin's DID configuration, you can easily determine which DIDs are associated with a particular origin. You can find more details about this at `https://identity.foundation/.well-known/resources/did-configuration/`.

Universal Resolver and Registrar

As I mentioned in earlier sections, a universal resolver is a critical component that allows applications to resolve DIDs across different DID systems. It provides a universal method for looking up DIDs, regardless of their underlying technology. A universal registrar complements this by offering a means to register DIDs in a standardized manner. You can find more details at `https://github.com/decentralized-identity/universal-resolver`.

Identity Hubs

As I mentioned earlier, identity hubs are user-controlled, off-chain personal datastores that play a vital role in managing identity data and enabling secure interaction. You can find this specification at `https://identity.foundation/decentralized-web-node/spec/0.0.1-predraft/`.

Sidetree Protocol

The Sidetree Protocol is a blockchain-agnostic protocol designed to support scalable and efficient DID operations on distributed ledgers. It allows for the creation, update, and resolution of DIDs in a way that minimizes on-chain transactions. The primary goals and features of this protocol are scalability, compatibility, global unique identifiers, user-controlled metadata, decentralization, and permissionless (without requiring trusted intermediaries, centralized authorities, special tokens or secondary consensus mechanism). You can find more details about this protocol at `https://identity.foundation/sidetree/spec/`.

DID Self-Issued OpenID

DID Self-Issued OpenID (SIOP) is focused on enabling secure and privacy-preserving authentication and authorization flows using decentralized identifiers. You can find the specification at `https://identity.foundation/did-siop/`.

Challenges and the Future Landscape

Decentralization will revolutionize how we manage digital identities and business. It offers greater control, privacy, and security to individuals. However, it also has lots of challenges such as standardization, adoption, scalability, and socialization across industries and across countries.

To unlock the full potential of decentralized identities, we need collaboration among stakeholders. This includes global leaders, industry leaders, organizations, regulatory bodies, and actual users. More interoperable standards and protocols must be developed to ensure that decentralized identity systems can seamlessly work together. By establishing a common language and framework, the industry can facilitate the widespread adoption of decentralized identity solutions. The DIF community is working toward creating a specifications, but it will require support and time.

Summary

This chapter provided an in-depth explanation of the transformative realm of decentralized digital identity management. The chapter opened with the new paradigm of identity, examining the shift from a traditional, centralized model to a decentralized model. Also, it delved into the importance of SSIs and highlighted how SSIs empower individuals with control over their identities. The chapter outlined the SSI principles, such as user autonomy and privacy, and also explained the benefits and challenges of SSI. The chapter covered how blockchain underpins the trust and security in decentralized identities and illustrated its function in automating and securing identity-related transactions. The chapter also detailed how decentralized systems will work in a real-world scenario and discussed trust mechanisms. Finally, the chapter highlighted the importance of universal frameworks for seamless integration.

CHAPTER 6

Cross Border Travel with Decentralized Identity

The World Economic Forum (WEF) and its partners have joined together under the project name "Shaping the Future of Security in Travel" to address the challenges of creating a seamless and secure travel experience. A solution has emerged through a thoughtful and travel-centric approach that involved mapping the entire traveler journey.

The technology involves biometric, blockchain, cryptography, and mobile devices to address seamless travel across borders. This decentralized control allows travelers to securely transmit proof of their identity, safeguarding the information using distributed ledger technology and cryptography both at the government level and through private-sector entities along the journey.

In this chapter, you will learn about seamless travel topics such as the following:

- The process involved in a decentralized journey

- Introduction to traveler digital identities

- The technical foundation of a traveler platform

- A distributed traveler infrastructure

- A distributed traveler architecture blueprint

- A global security framework for a traveler platform

© Shivakumar R. Goniwada 2024
S. R. Goniwada, *Introduction to One Digital Identity*, https://doi.org/10.1007/979-8-8688-0255-3_6

Introduction to Seamless Travel Across Borders

The global economy often requires people to cross country borders, especially within the business and tourism industries. These industries play a crucial role in facilitating the safe and efficient transportation of more than approximately 6 million individuals daily, according to U.S. airline traffic data.

Historically, travel was a luxury accessible primarily to the affluent. Today there is a flourishing tourism sector. These developments, coupled with the growth of disposable income, the rise of the middle class and emerging markets, and the shift of societal attitude toward travel, have paved the way for a surge in international travel.

The technological advancements in the field of digital identity with biometrics and blockchain/ledger technologies present a wealth of opportunities to revolutionize and strengthen the global travel security system. These innovations have the potential to enhance both the efficiency and the effectiveness of security in global travel. However, it's essential to recognize that while technology can be powerful, individuals with malicious intent can also exploit it, so technology advancement cannot alone address the complex security challenges.

Having said that, the World Economic Forum (WEF) has initiated a project for fostering open dialogue and is acting as an impartial moderator in addressing the challenges such as consensus across all countries, security measures, platform, etc. Without the WEF, digital cross-border technology would not be possible. This platform is called the Known Traveler Digital Identity (KTDI).

A related concept is *identity proofing*, which is a critical process to ensure that an individual's claimed identity matches their actual identity. This is a common experience in everyday situations such as checking into a hotel, where you need to show identification to verify your identity. Despite its ubiquity, identity proofing is often perceived as burdensome and invasive. However, its importance cannot be overstated, especially in light of the staggering number of identity thefts and fraud reported annually.

Cross-Border Travel

Cross-border travel involves specific stages that a traveler goes through. As shown in Figure 6-1, a typical travel process includes various checkpoints and procedures to ensure the safe movement of individuals from one country to another.

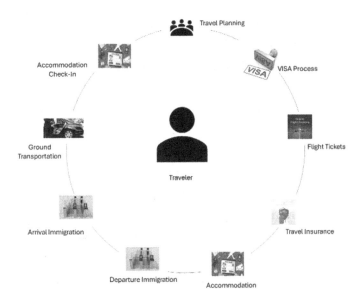

Figure 6-1. *Cross-border travel process*

The Role of Identity in Travel

Identity plays a central and multifaceted role in the realm of travel. It encompasses various aspects that are essential for both individuals and authorities responsible for facilitating safe and efficient international travel.

Passports and visas have long been the primary means of establishing your identity and the eligibility of your international travel. These documents serve as physical proof of nationality and authorization. Modern identity verification increasingly relies on biometric data such as fingerprints, facial recognition, and/or iris scans.

Accurate identity verification is fundamental to national security. Authorities at borders use identity checks to screen individuals for potential threats or criminal activities, and respective governments keep records of a traveler's entry and exit, helping to monitor visa compliance and immigration patterns.

In addition, airlines, hotels, and car rental companies require identity information for reservations and check-in, and many travel companies offer loyalty programs that rely on customer identity to provide personalized services and rewards.

Decentralized identity plays a crucial role in the travel industry by redefining how you prove your identity, share personal information, and navigate the intricacies of international travel. As I mentioned in Chapter 6, decentralized identity empowers you with unprecedented control over your data through the principle of self-sovereign identity (SSI). You hold your digital identities and determine when, where, and with whom you share specific information, granting consent for identity verification.

Decentralized systems are expected to revolutionize how we verify our identity while traveling. These systems are designed to be interoperable, meaning they can work smoothly across different travel-related entities such as airlines, immigration authorities, hotels, taxis, and travel insurance companies. Imagine carrying your digital identity on your smartphone or having a specialized travel chip issued by your country of residence that contains all your travel-related documents securely stored in the user agents and blockchain. Instead of carrying multiple physical documents or going through the lengthy verification processes at each point of your journey, you'd simply use your digital identity stored on your smartphone or chip. This would make travel streamlined, secure, and convenient, as your identity and travel documents could be quickly and securely verified at every step of your journey, from boarding a flight to checking into a hotel.

Traveler Digital Identities

Digital identities represent a fundamental shift in how identity and verification and traveler information sharing are approached in the context of travel. A traveler digital identity is designed to enhance both security and convenience for travelers while enabling more efficient and effective processes for law enforcement, immigration, and aviation security officials.

In addition, digital identities allow authorities to request and receive the verified traveler information much earlier in the journey when planning and booking processes. This early access to information enables a redesign of security processes, emphasizing advanced passenger screening and expedited clearance of low-risk travelers. By receiving traveler data earlier, authorities can prioritize their efforts to vet passengers who are less familiar or raise security concerns.

Travelers can selectively share biometric, biographic, and travel history data with relevant authorities and private-sector entities such as immigration, hotels, airlines, and car rental agencies, and travelers can tailor the information by sharing only specific details with each authority or service provider. This privacy and security.

E-Passports

E-passports are a significant advancement in border management and travel facilitation. They utilize a contactless chip containing the passport holder's biographical data and digital security features in the form of a digital signature. This digital signature plays a crucial role in ensuring the integrity and authenticity of the passport.

The chip in the e-passport allows border authorities to electronically validate the integrity of the document and use the digital signature to verify the authenticity of the e-passport including details such as issuing authority, place, issued date, expiration date, name, surname, and address.

The International Civil Aviation Organization Public Key Directory (ICAO PKD)[1] serves as a trusted global source for facilitating the exchange of digital certificate chain information and is the decentralized identity that will be linked to this directory.

E-Visas

E-visas represent a transformative shift in how countries manage entry and security for international travelers. These automated systems play a pivotal role in determining the eligibility of individuals to visit a particular country from a security perspective. The decentralization adds extra and granular-based systems to validate the e-visas.

A decentralized digital identity adds an e-visa attestation to the individual's decentralized store by integrating consulate offices, which can significantly improve the efficiency and security of travel, as shown in Figure 6-2.

---

[1] icao.int/Security/FAL/PKD/Pages/ePassport-Basics.aspx

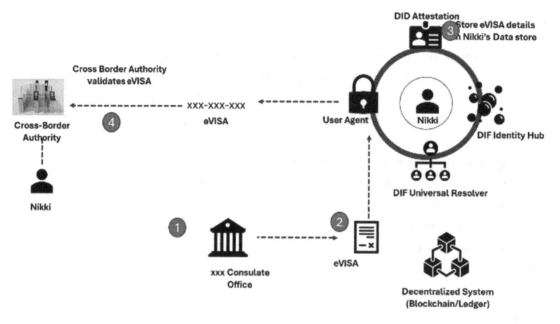

Figure 6-2. *E-visa process*

Let's consider an example. Nikki would like to travel to the Netherlands for leisure, and she requires a visa, so she has enrolled herself in the decentralized digital identity platform. To get an e-visa, she has to follow these steps:

- Consulate offices will provide Nikki with the information to create a decentralized identity visa as part of the visa application process.

- Nikki travels to the Netherlands consulate in her own country to undergo identity verification, including a biometric data capture to ensure the authenticity of her digital identity.

- Once the digital identity is created and verified, it becomes the primary source of identity information for visa-related transactions.

- Nikki can use her digital identity to fill out visa application forms online at the consulate office.

- The consulate office will use Nikki's digital identity to verify the details before issuing the visa. Once the visa approved by the authorities, it needs to be electronically signed and issued to Nikki's digital identity.

- At the cross-border gate, Nikki can give her digital identity information to authorities to verify her authenticity and eligibility.

In this process, Nikki, the consulate office, and the immigration authority work together as part of the decentralized identity with blockchain/ledger technology.

Current Technology and Digitization Enablement

Technology is being used in the travel industry more than ever before. Airline travelers are able to book flights, select seats, and check in online, which reduces the time spent in airports. This digitization makes the pre-travel experience more convenient.

In addition, boarding passes stored on smartphones eliminate the need for paper tickets, making the boarding processes smoother and more eco-friendly. Automated passport control and immigration clearance gates use biometrics and digital identity verification to expedite entry and exit procedures. Currently, there are many airlines around the world using this process.

In fact, many airports have embraced technology in the form of automated gates, which leverage advanced biometric capabilities encompassing both physical and behavioral recognition. These gates offer a myriad of advantages, fundamentally transforming airport security and passenger facilitation. There is transparency, as passengers can witness the process, which fosters trust and confidence in the security measures.

As you can see, the aviation industry has embraced technology in general, and integration with decentralized identity technology will help the industry further improve the passengers' experience.

Technical Foundations for a Traveler Platform

Decentralized digital identities have the potential to revolutionize the travel industry. A digital identity represents a significant advancement in the way you manage your trusted and verified identity attributes. This approach relies on a combination of cryptography, distributed ledger technology, and emerging international standards to empower you to self-manage your digital identities securely.

Attestation, in the traveler context, is provided by entities like government passport agencies and consulates. These attestations serve as proof of specific identity attributes, such as citizenship or travel history. The more attestations you accumulate, the more known they become in the system. This is like a CBIL score for banking transactions in India or the credit scoring system in the United States, Canda, Japan, UK, and

China. This trust and reputation-building process enables individualized, risk-based differentiation in border management and aviation security screening.

The digital identity system is designed to be travel-centric, empowering you to securely manage all the attestations and other details on your mobile device or chips. With this, you have control over sharing the attestations with the relevant entities.

From a security agency perspective, the digital identity system provides security agencies with early access to reliable and verified information about you before you arrive at the border checkpoint. This information allows security agencies to scrutinize traveler information and redirect their attention away from known, low-risk passengers to instead focus on less-known travelers who may pose security risks.

Design Principles

The development of a traveler digital identity platform, centered around on the principles of SSI, emphasizes the importance of user control and autonomy over data. The concept details entails four core design principles: personal, portable, private, and persistent. These principles are essential in designing a secure and user-centric digital identity system for travelers.

- **Personal:** The traveler data and identity are owned and controlled by the individual traveler, ensuring that they are the authority of their data. To achieve this, the platform must use a decentralized identity solution that relies on blockchain or distributed ledger technology and enables travelers to create and manage digital identities independently.

- **Portable:** Travelers' data and credentials are easily accessible and transferable across various services and borders. The platform must use interoperable standards and protocols to ensure that it can seamlessly work across different travel services and regions, enhancing portability. The W3C is creating a specification and standards for interoperable and protocols.

- **Private:** A traveler's privacy is prioritized, and personal data is disclosed only on a need-to-known basis, preserving confidentiality. The platform must use cryptographic techniques such as zero-knowledge proofs, enable privacy-preserving verification, and allow for secure credentials verification without exposing sensitive information.

- **Persistent:** Travelers' identities and credentials need to be consistent and available over time, even when upgrading or changing devices. The platform must use distributed technology, which underpins the decentralized identity, to ensure the persistence and immutability of traveler data and prevent data loss and tampering.

Core Technologies

A traveler platform relies on core technologies that provide the foundation of its secure and user-centric design.

- **Distributed ledger technology (DLT):** DLT allows for the secure and transparent sharing of data across a network of computers. It is the underlying technology behind the blockchain and plays a crucial role in establishing trust in the platform network without the need for a centralized authority. DLT represents a decentralized and tamper-resistant data structure, where information is replicated, shared, and synchronized across multiple geographical locations, countries, or institutions. This network operates without a central administrative agency, functioning as a dedicated peer-to-peer network.

- **Public-private key cryptography:** This provides the necessary security for authorizing and sharing sensitive information. This helps to encrypt and decrypt data, and it uses two keys, a public key and a private key. The public key can be shared with anyone, and the private key is kept secret with you. In the platform, this will be used to authenticate individuals and to protect the privacy of your identity data.

- **Advanced biometrics:** The advanced biometrics as explained in Chapter 4, such as facial recognition and fingerprint scans, bridge the physical and digital realms by connecting a traveler's unique physical characteristics to their digital identity.

- **Mobile interface:** This serves as the primary interface for travelers to carry the digital identities and manage credentials.

While these core technologies are instrumental in realizing a traveler's platform, emerging technologies often lack a one-size-fits-all solution. Therefore, it is crucial to evaluate each technology. Along with these technologies, you need to consider data protection, privacy, regulations, usability, and accessibility of the users.

Decentralized Identity Infrastructure[2]

Building a decentralized identity infrastructure for travel is no different than with other digital identity infrastructures. The infrastructure requires collaboration from government agencies, technology providers, and travel-related organizations, and all these partners must have the ability to provide attestation on respective documents such as passports, visas, and tickets. Figure 6-3 shows the infrastructure.

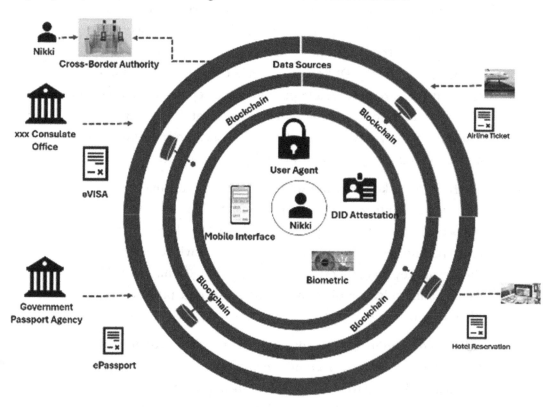

Figure 6-3. *Traveler platform with digital identities*

² https://ktdi.org/

The first pillar of the infrastructure is the blockchain. A decentralized platform uses blockchain technology to manage privacy and data efficiency. In Figure 6-3, the data is not stored in the actual blockchain; instead, the blockchain references the data of each agency and organization. These reference pointers enable authorized participants to access the associated identity data. These hubs store the data objects that are signed by an identity and are accessible via APIs.

The blockchain is linked to the distributed certificate authority, which maintains the mapping of identities to corresponding public keys. Furthermore, smart contracts are integrated into the blockchain.

The second pillar of the infrastructure is the public key infrastructure (PKI), which plays a crucial role in ensuring the secure digital authentication of documents such as e-visas and e-passports. As I mentioned, PKI works on the principle of public key cryptography, where security relies on a pair of cryptographic keys, a public key and a private key.

The third pillar is biometrics, which play a pivotal role in connecting a digital identity to the physical world. The digital authentication encompasses something you know, something you have, and something you are. The first two are passwords, PINs, etc. The third category uses biometrics as an authentication method. For example, the International Air Transport Association (IATA) is in the process of creating a transformative biometric for airport-specific and frictionless processes.

The fourth pillar is the mobile interface, which is one of the most convenient ways to carry a digital identity app. This interface generates private keys, transmits public keys to identity issuers, and stores digital records associated with the corresponding private keys or decentralized identifiers. The mobile identity app provides you with a comprehensive view of your digital identity components and a user-friendly interface through which you can share these attestations with both cross-border authorities and other government entities. The mobile interface must also contain the user consent for sharing personal information with recipients within a defined framework.

Traveler Architecture Blueprint

The fundamental architecture leverages the synergy of the four core technologies, as shown in Figure 6-4. The architecture needs to integrate with the live production system of all the required stakeholders within the travel ecosystem, such as government agencies, consulates, border agencies, aviation organizations, hospitality providers, and more.

In this architecture, the following happens:

- The distributed ledger is used to store pointers to the identity data of Nikki. This means the actual identity data is not stored in the blockchain but rather on other data sources, which helps to protect the privacy and security of identity data.[3]

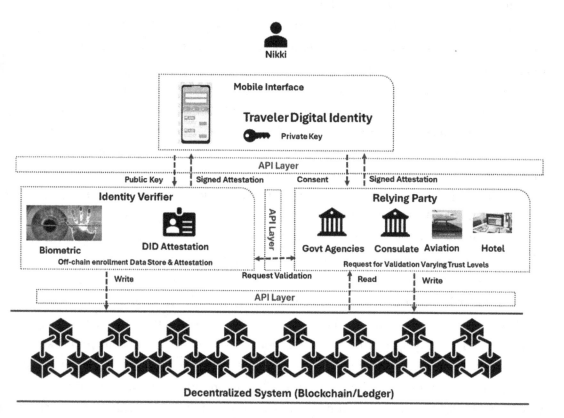

Figure 6-4. *Traveler architecture blueprint*

- Cryptography is used to secure the identity data to authenticate Nikki. This includes using public-key cryptography to sign and verify digital identity documents and using encryption to protect the data in transit and at rest .

- Biometrics are used to identify Nikki's travel. Nikki's stored fingerprint, face, or iris scan is used for authentication.

---

[3] https://ktdi.org/

- The mobile interface enables Nikki to carry an app to share and store the private key.

- All the components communicate with the API through a secured API gateway.

In summary, Nikki registers her identity data with the trusted decentralized identity provider, and her identity is stored on a distributed ledger platform along with a pointer to a hub where the actual identity data is stored. Once this is done, Nikki can use a mobile interface to access the application to share her identity with other entities. When Nikki shares her identity, the other entities can use the pointer in the distributed ledger to access Nikki's identity hub from the overall hub. The other entities can verify Nikki's identity using her biometric data.

Identity Proofing

Identity proofing is the process that verifies a user's identity, which goes beyond the typical username/password authentication system. It's a critical step either before a user is granted access credentials to an application or as a parallel measure to traditional authentication methods. These are the two key guidelines outlined by the National Institute of Standards and Technology (NIST) in its digital identity guidelines:

- **Claimed identity:** This is the information a user provides when registering with a decentralized identity system; it represents the identity the user claims to possess.

- **Actual identity:** This refers to the verified data that confirms the authenticity of the user's identity, proving who they actually are.

The primary objective of identity proofing is to match the user's claimed identity with their actual identity (verified against any government-issued identity), ensuring that the identity they present is not fictitious or fraudulent. By effectively confirming that a user is genuinely who they claim to be, identity proofing acts as a frontline defense against identity theft, unauthorized access, and other related cybercrimes.

The NIST outlines three essential steps in the identity proofing process. These steps are designed to establish and confirm a user's identity with accuracy and reliability.

- **Resolution:** This step involves distinguishing a person's identity within the specific context of a system. It's about identifying the individual from among all the other users or entities in the system. Resolution is crucial because it ensures that each identity within the system is unique. This step prevents identity overlap and ensures that each user has a separate, identifiable presence within the system.

- **Validation:** The process involves collecting identifying information from the user. This might include biometric details or a simple username/password. This step confirms the accuracy of the information collected.

- **Verification:** This process is about verifying that the user is indeed who they claim to be. Verification is often the most critical part of the process, where the information provided in the validation stage is used to confirm the user's identity. This might involve cross-checking against external databases, using biometric data, or using any other available advanced techniques.

Global Travel Security Framework

The effectiveness of various technological solutions in enhancing global travel security can be fully realized only through a coordinated and collaborative approach among nations. It is evident that a cohesive global framework is essential to establish standardized security protocols that organizations like the International Civil Aviation Organization (ICAO) can endorse. This blueprint would guide nations globally in adopting and adhering to security standards, facilitating the exchange of traveler data across borders, streamlining security processes to counter potential threats, and ensuring the smooth flow of people across borders.

Furthermore, fostering greater cooperation and information sharing among nations is imperative to address the combat global security challenges effectively. This includes sharing intelligence, threat details, and data that can be identified and mitigate potential risks, as shown in Figure 6-5.

- **Common unified identity authentication:** Establishing a unified identity authentication system for individuals crossing international borders can streamline security procedures while maintaining a high level of trust and verification.

- **Using e-visas and -passports and participation from other organizations:** The integration of e-visas and e-passports can expedite the entry and border clearance process, and nations must issue an e-visa and e-passport for all participants and collaborate globally on the network.

- **Regulations and standards:** The W3C and other organizations are creating standards that every nation must adapt. The World Economic Forum along with partner nations must create a regulatory framework that is to be adopted by all the nations.

- **Unified common network security:** This network emphasizes the importance of adopting and implementing common network security around the world.

- **Unified global database:** Access to a global criminal database can aid in identifying and tracking individuals with criminal records or those deemed potential security risks, contributing to enhanced security measures.

- **Law enforcement:** Strengthening collaboration among law enforcement agencies across borders is crucial for addressing transactional security threats and criminal activities effectively.

- **Unified global security standards:** This capability emphasizes the importance of adopting and implementing consistent and harmonized data security standards globally, ensuring that sensitive traveler information is adequately protected.

Figure 6-5. *Global security framework*

While the implementation of these framework elements on a global scale may be a medium to long-term aspiration, nations should consider initiating such frameworks at the regional level to kickstart the process and build momentum. Regional integration efforts can serve as a testing ground for these security measures, helping refine and scale up the program for broader adoption. Global tourism working groups and multinational organizations can play a pivotal role in facilitating regional approaches to travel security. These organizations can serve as platforms for dialogue, cooperation, and the development of regional security initiatives for a safer efficient global travel environment.

Travel Risk Management[4]

ISO 31030:2021 provides a set of standards and guidelines to organizations for when their employees travel domestically or internationally. Travelers often encounter varying risk profiles due to factors such as road accidents, disease outbreaks, natural

---

[4] https://www.iso.org/obp/ui/en/#iso:std:iso:31030:ed-1:v1:en

disasters, conflict, crime, cyber threats, terrorism, and political instability. These risks can threaten not only their physical safety and health but also their information security and mental well-being, potentially jeopardizing the success of their travel objectives. The effectiveness of travel risk management (TRM) hinges on the timeliness and accuracy of intelligence, including travel warnings, which play a pivotal role in making informed decisions.

Summary

This chapter provided a comprehensive overview of the evolving landscape of cross-border travel in the context of digital identity. This chapter introduced how digital transformation is reshaping travel and examined the cross-border process. This included an exploration of the role of identity in the travel journey process, highlighting how a traveler's digital identity simplifies and secures international movement. The chapter then delved into the present-day technologies and role of digitization enabling these changes, laying out the technical foundation required for a robust traveler platform. Key design principles and core technologies were discussed, emphasizing the importance of a decentralized identity infrastructure that aligns with SSI values. The architecture blueprint for such a traveler's system was outlined, illustrating how it can be built and integrated. Furthermore, identity proofing was covered, including how it ensures the authenticity and security of traveler identities. The chapter wrapped up with a discussion of the global travel security framework, addressing the border implications and requirements for ensuring safe and secure travel in this digitally interconnected world. This comprehensive approach illustrates the significance of digital identity in transforming cross-border travel, making it more efficient, secure, and user-friendly.

CHAPTER 7

Social Media with Decentralized Identity

A social media evolution is underway, driven by the emergence of decentralized identities. This transition from a centralized to a decentralized identity system has the potential to revolutionize the way the individuals interact, manage their personal data, and engage with various entities in the digital world. This chapter delves into the intricacies of decentralized identities in the context of social media, exploring the architecture, platforms, benefits, and challenges.

In this chapter, you will learn about the following:

- Challenges of current social media platforms

- The technology and architecture of decentralized social media platforms

- Challenges in distributed identity social media platforms

- Revolutionary features of decentralized social media platforms

Introduction to Social Media Identities

Social media platforms have become integral to our lives, serving as the primary channel for communication, networking, and self-expression on the Internet. As we know by now, the issues of social media are privacy, security, and control of our personal data. This is where decentralization comes into play, offering a compelling and timely solution.

Digital identities hold immense relevance in the realm of social media because of its capacity to address critical issues that have emerged with the widespread adoption of these platforms. First, a decentralized identity addresses the vulnerabilities inherent

© Shivakumar R. Goniwada 2024
S. R. Goniwada, *Introduction to One Digital Identity*, https://doi.org/10.1007/979-8-8688-0255-3_7

in centralized identity management systems, where you often surrender control of your personal information to a single social media platform, resulting in potential data breaches and misuse. Moreover, concerns regarding data privacy, user consent, and the safeguarding of personal information underscore the pressing need for the integration of decentralized identities on social media platforms.

By enabling you to take control of your digital identities, decentralization empowers you with self-sovereignty, ensuring that you determine how and when your data is shared across various social media platforms. The decentralized identity provides enhanced security, privacy, and user agency, thus reshaping the dynamics of trust and accountability in the digital space.

The Evolution of Social Media

The evolution of social media has been rapid and transformative, beginning as a simple platform for direct electronic information exchange. It quickly evolved into a virtual gathering space, where people could connect and share information with family and friends. Early platforms like Friendster and MySpace were catalysts for this transformation, and they laid the groundwork for the more complex and far-reaching platforms like Facebook (Meta), Twitter (X), and Instagram. As these platforms grew, they incorporated more features, turning into hubs for news, entertainment, and advertising. This shift marked social media's emergence as a retail platform, revolutionizing how products and services are marketed and sold online.

The impact of social media on the lives of billions has been profound. It has reshaped how people communicate, access information, and form opinions, often blurring the lines between personal and public spheres. Social media has also been a catalyst for significant social and political movements, enabling the rapid spread of information (and misinformation) and the mobilization of people across the globe.

For business, the rise of a digital consumer lifestyle meant adapting to a new way to engage customers. Traditional marketing strategies were overhauled to prioritize digital channels, with a particular focus on leveraging social media's vast reach and influence. Companies now use these platforms for targeted advertising, brand building, customer engagement, and more.

Centralized, Decentralized, Federated, and Distributed Social Networks

Let's look at the different types of social networks.

Centralized Social Networks

Centralized network platforms such as Facebook (Meta) and Twitter (X) are operated by a single corporate entity that maintains complete control over the network's infrastructure and operations. In this model, all user data and interactions are stored and processed on servers owned and managed by that single company. This centralization allows for a uniform streamlined user experience, as the company can efficiently implement and update features, moderate content, and manage network traffic.

However, this concentration of control also raises significant concerns. First, it places a vast amount of personal data under the purview of a single entity, potentially jeopardizing user privacy. The company's decisions on data use, storage, and sharing directly impacts millions of users. Additionally, content regulation policies are solely determined by the company, sometimes leading to accusations of bias or censorship.

Decentralized Social Networks

A decentralized social network represents a shift from the traditional, centralized model of social media platforms. In a decentralized social network, control and data storage are distributed across multiple independent nodes rather than being centralized in the hands of a single entity. This means that no single node has overarching control over the entire network, which significantly enhances user privacy and reduces the risk of widespread censorship. Each node operates autonomously, hosted on its own set of user data and content.

This decentralization inherently protects against the risk associated with a single point of failure and centralized control, making the network more resilient to outages and external manipulation. The challenges are that not having a central authority can lead to variations in the user experience, as different nodes might have different interfaces, features, and performance levels.

141

Federated Social Networks

Federated social networks represent a unique blend of decentralization and some elements of centralization, creating a network comprised of multiple independent nodes, each operating its own mini-network. These servers are capable of communicating with each other, akin to how different email servers interact. In this network, users are typically registered on a specific server, but they can interact and share content with users on other servers within the same federation. This structure allows for a diversity of communities and governance models, as each server can establish its own rules, moderation policies, and cultural norms, reflecting the preferences and needs of its user base.

Despite this independence, the federated model maintains a level of interconnectedness that allows for a broader social experience across different servers. It strikes a balance between giving individual servers the freedom to control their environment, while still enabling a unified and cohesive user experience across the wider network. This approach addresses some of the privacy and control concerns inherent in fully centralized networks, offering users a more diverse and potentially more secure environment.

Distributed Social Networks

Distributed social networks represent the epitome of decentralization in the digital world, eliminating the concept of a central server completely. Operating on a peer-to-peer (P2P) model, each user's device functions as an independent node, collectively forming the network's infrastructure. This approach to network design ensures that the data and control are not centralized in any single location, significantly enhancing privacy and making the network highly resistant to censorship and external control. This structure inherently protects user data from being monopolized or misused by a central authority.

Decentralized Social Media

The shift toward decentralized social media platforms is driven by several factors that reflect the growing user concerns and limitations of current centralized platforms. The limitations are data privacy and ownership, freedom over the user content, trust and transparency, security concerns, and user empowerment and interoperability.

- There are privacy and ownership concerns because the present-day centralized platforms are controlled by corporations that collect and possibly misuse user data.

- Freedom over user content means users on a decentralized platform can enjoy a more unfiltered and unbiased content experience. Without the influence of centralized content moderation policies or algorithmic biases that typically shape user feeds in centralized networks, users have more control over the content they see and share.

- Currently, the trust and transparency in centralized social network platforms are minimal. A decentralized platform restores the trust by providing a verifiable and immutable record of interactions and data exchanges.

- You have probably read or heard of data breaches across many platforms; this is because the centralized platforms are vulnerable to breaches. Decentralized platforms are more secure against data breaches as the data is distributed across different networks.

- Decentralized social networks are aligned with a broader principle of Web 3.0, which emphasizes user empowerment because the user has more control over their user identities.

Decentralized social media, inspired by blockchain principles, marks a shift from traditional social media's way of storing data. Typically, social media platforms keep all their data in one central location, which is risky because if hackers break into this one spot, they could access a lot of user information. Decentralized platforms, on the other hand, use a network of many connected points, called *nodes*. If one node is compromised, the others remain secure, making it much less likely that a single hack could provide access a lot of user data. This way of distributing data across multiple points can greatly improve security, reducing the danger that comes from relying on a single storage point.

One of the fundamental advantages of this approach is the inherent immutability of and tamper-resistant nature of blockchain technology. Data stored on a blockchain (either on-chain or off-chain) is practically invulnerable to unauthorized manipulation or alteration. This unique feature acts as a safeguard, creating a more secure environment for data. At its core, the decentralization movement seeks to democratize digital identities. In the emerging Web 3.0 paradigm, the emphasis is on giving individuals control and ownership over digital personas, leading to a higher level of security and privacy.

There are various decentralized platforms already available; they are covered next.

Nostr

Nostr is a decentralized Web 3.0 social media platform leveraging decentralization to enhance privacy and security. Unlike popular present-day social media, Nostr operates without central servers and in a decentralized network. The users are identified by their public keys instead of user personas. This makes tracking and impersonation more challenging. The use of public/private key pairs in Nostr accounts embodies a core principle of decentralized identity systems, where the public key acts as the username and the private key as a password. Here the username and password comparison is just conceptual, because the private key cannot be recovered, but passwords can be. You can find more details about this platform at `https://nostr.com/`.

Mastodon

Mastodon is a decentralized social networking platform unlike Twitter or Facebook. It accommodates diverse content creation, similar to other platforms. However, its chronological feed is a significant deviation from the algorithmically curated timeline that dominates other platforms. You can find more details at `https://joinmastodon.org/`.

There are a growing number of decentralized social media platforms available; these are just examples. The shift from centralized to decentralized is part of the broader trend toward a more open platform. The shift to a decentralized social media platform is still in its early stages, but it has the potential to create a more equitable and secure online environment. As more people become aware of the benefits of decentralized platforms, we can expect to see their popularity grow.

Designing and Implementing Decentralized Identities for Social Media

Designing a decentralized social media platform requires a careful balance of several critical factors, each intertwined to ensure that the platform is resilient, is user-friendly, and respects the autonomy of its users. First, user control and privacy must be at the core of the platform's design philosophy. This means that users are the custodian of their personal data, with a transparent mechanism in place that allows them to grant or revoke access permissions and manage how information is shared and utilized.

For security and data integrity, leveraging blockchain's inherent capabilities is crucial; these include cryptographic encryption, decentralized consensus mechanisms, and tamper-evident ledgers for auditability. These measures are vital in protecting user data from unauthorized access and ensuring that once information is recorded, it cannot be altered without consensus.

Scalability and performance are often challenges in decentralized networks, given their distributed nature. The platform must be designed to handle the growing numbers of users and the high volume of transactions. Interoperability is essential for a decentralized platform to thrive within the ecosystem. The platform must be based on open protocols and standards, allowing easy integration with other platforms.

Architectural Overview of Decentralized Social Media Platforms

The architectural components of decentralized social media platforms represent a paradigm shift from traditional, centralized social media platforms. There are several components in decentralized social media platforms that work together to create a more democratic, user-driven environment. The following are the crucial components.

Storage

Unlike centralized platforms, where all the user data is stored in a single location, decentralized social media platforms take a different approach by storing data across a network of multiple nodes; they do this using distributed ledger technology, commonly known as the *blockchain*. In this setup, each node in the network holds a copy of the ledger, which records all transactions or data exchanges on the platform. This means that instead of having one central point that stores all the information, the data is spread out and duplicated across many different locations. Each of these nodes works together to validate and record new data, making the system more secure. If one node is compromised, the others can still maintain the integrity of the data.

Moreover, this decentralized structure makes it very hard for any single entity to control or manipulate the information, enhancing user privacy and security. It also offers more resistance to censorship, as there is no central authority that can easily remove or block content. This blockchain-based approach represents a significant shift from traditional social media, promising greater security and control for users over their data.

Communication

In a decentralized network, where data is distributed across various nodes, these nodes communicate directly with each other to exchange data and manage the network. Each node represents an individual point in the network, like a computer or server, holding a copy of the network's data or ledger. This direct communication is key to maintaining the network's integrity and functionality. When a change or update occurs, such as adding new data or validating transactions, this information is shared among the nodes. The nodes work collaboratively to verify the accuracy of the new data, a process that often involves complex algorithms or consensus mechanisms to ensure all nodes agree on the network's current state. This decentralized approach eliminates the need for a central authority to oversee and manage the network, making it more resilient and secure. If one node fails or is compromised, the others can continue to operate, preserving the network's continuity. Furthermore, this direct node-to-node communication enhances the network's ability to resist censorship and external control, as there is no single point where data exchange can be easily interrupted or manipulated. This self-managing and cooperative nature of nodes is a fundamental aspect of decentralized networks, enabling them to operate securely and efficiently.

Content Curation

In decentralized social networks, the role of users in determining content visibility is markedly different from that in centralized social networks. Here, users have a more direct influence over what content is displayed, either through their interactions, such as likes, shares, and comments, or through preferences set within the network's algorithms. Unlike centralized platforms, where algorithms are often proprietary and operate in opaque ways, decentralized networks tend to offer greater transparency in how content is curated and prioritized. This transparency allows users to understand and potentially influence the mechanics behind content distribution. Furthermore, since these networks are not driven by the same commercial imperatives as many centralized platforms, there's typically less emphasis on addictive content or engagement-driven algorithms that can skew what is seen and shared. Instead, the focus is more on reflecting the genuine preferences and interest of the community. The user-driven approach not only empowers individuals but also fosters a more diverse and organic content ecosystem, where the visibility of posts is more a reflection of the community's values and choices rather than the strategic goals of a centralized authority. This structure can lead to a more democratic and equitable information-sharing environment, aligning closely with the ethos of decentralization.

Moderation

Moderation on decentralized platforms takes a distinctly different approach compared to centralized social networks, leaning toward community-led initiatives. In this model, the power to decide what is deemed appropriate or harmful content is largely in the hands of the users themselves, rather than a centralized authority. This democratic approach to content moderation is facilitated by various tools and mechanisms, some of which are still in development, to help communities self-regulate. These tools can include voting systems, where users collectively decide on the visibility or appropriateness of content, or reputation-based systems, where the influence of a user's moderation decisions is tied to their standing within the community.

Additionally, decentralized platforms may employ algorithms that users can customize to filter content according to their preferences, rather than relying on a one-size-fits-all approach. While this decentralized approach to moderation empowers users and can lead to a more diverse and open environment, it also presents challenges. Ensuring consistent enforcement of community standards and combating harmful content effectively can be more complex when the responsibility is distributed among a large and varied group of users. Nevertheless, as these tools evolve, they offer the potential for a more inclusive and representation system of content moderation, in line with the decentralized ethos of these platforms.

Governance

In decentralized social networks, governance adopts a more democratic and participatory model, contrasting sharply with the top-down decision-making typical of centralized platforms. Here decisions about network rules, policies, and future developments are often made through voting or consensus mechanisms involving the users or nodes themselves. This approach ensures that the users, who are the backbone of the network, have a significant say in its governance. For instance, changes in the platform's protocol, moderation policies, or feature updates can be subject to community votes, where each user's voice contributes to the final decision.

Similarly, nodes in the network might participate in consensus mechanisms, especially in blockchain-based platforms, where they validate transactions or changes based on agreed-upon protocols. This decentralized governance model fosters a sense of ownership and accountability among users, as the network evolves based on collective input and agreement. It's designed to reflect the community's interests and values more accurately, leading to more equitable and representative management of the platform.

However, this model also faces challenges, such as achieving broad participation, ensuring informed voting, and managing diverse opinions to reach consensus.

Decentralized Platform (Mastodon) Architecture

In this section, I'll explain the decentralized platform of Mastodon. The concept of Mastodon is similar to Twitter/X. You can post short messages, which are visible to your followers, and you or your followers can retweet or like messages.

Twitter/X operates as a centralized platform, meaning it is controlled and maintained by a single entity: X. This includes the management of servers, algorithms, data storage, moderation policy, governance, and user accounts. On Twitter, all the users abide by the same set of rules and algorithms set by the platform, leading to a uniform user experience for all its users.

Mastodon is different from Twitter; it consists of numerous independent instances, or servers. Each instance operates like a small-scale Twitter, with its own user base, governance, and moderation rules. Despite being independent, these instances are not isolated. They are part of a federation network, allowing them to communicate and exchange data each other. Users of one Mastodon instance can easily follow and interact with users from other instance. This enables a broader, network-wide interaction while maintaining the unique characteristics of each instance.

Let's look at the decentralized Mastodon architecture; Figure 7-1 shows a simplified version of it.

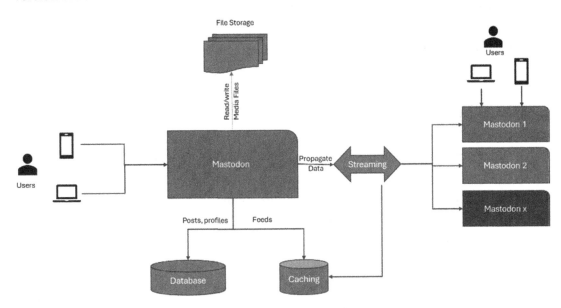

Figure 7-1. *Mastodon decentralized architecture*

In this architecture, the database is used to manage profiles and posts, caching is used for feeds and jobs, and file storage is used to store files such as photos.

When you create posts on Mastodon, they are first stored in a database, which acts as a primary data store for your Mastodon instance. A post is then added to the home feeds of your local followers that are present in the same instance of Mastodon ("Mastodon" in the figure). The home feeds are stored in the cache. If you have followers on another Mastodon server, your posts are propagated to those Mastodon servers ("Mastodon 1," "Mastodon 2," or "Mastodon x" in the figure). The post is propagated to the other Mastodon servers depending on your follower base; for example, if you have 10 followers and they are residing on separate Mastodon servers (1–10), then your Mastodon server propagates 10 jobs from your Mastodon server and publishes the post. You can find more details in the Mastodon documentation.[1]

---

[1] https://docs.joinmastodon.org/

Integration with DIDs

At the time of writing this book, Mastodon does not have native support for DIDs, but there are potential ways they could be integrated in the future.

One approach is through DID authentication plugins. Engineers could create these plugins for Mastodon servers, allowing users to log in using their DIDs instead of the traditional username and password combination. This integration would necessitate compatibility with specific DID protocols and standards, ensuring secure and seamless authentication processes.

Another potential integration is using DIDs for profile verification. In this scenario, DIDs could authenticate and verify the identities of individuals or organizations on Mastodon, perhaps by displaying verified claims about the owner, such as links to the website or verified social media accounts. This could enhance trust and credibility within the network.

Lastly, social graphs powered by the CyberConnect protocol could leverage DIDs. This would involve storing connections and interactions on a blockchain or another type of distributed ledger, rather than Mastodon's servers. Such an approach could bolster privacy and give users greater control over their social networking data.

Technical Challenges and Impact

Implementing decentralization in social media brings its own set of challenges.

Scalability

One of the main challenges is managing a large user base and handling high transaction volumes. In decentralized systems, as the number of nodes and transactions increases, maintaining efficiency and speed can become difficult. This can lead to slower transaction times and reduced responsiveness, which impacts the user experience.

Regulations

Navigating the complex legal and regulatory landscape can be especially challenging for decentralized platforms. The lack of a central controlling entity can create ambiguity in legal responsibilities and compliance. This can result in difficulties gaining legal acceptance, impacting the platform's ability to operate in certain jurisdictions.

User Experience

A decentralized network consists of various independent nodes or communities, each with its own focus and user base. This fragmentation could make it difficult for users to discover and connect with others outside their immediate community.

Server Providers

Decentralized platforms often rely on external server providers for hosting various nodes of the network. This reliance introduces points of vulnerability. If the server provider faces downtime or a security breach, it can impact the availability and integrity of the platform.

Governance

Governance in decentralized social networks presents a unique set of challenges due to its community-driven nature. Unlike centralized platforms where decision-making is streamlined through a central authority, decentralized networks often rely on consensus among community members.

Decentralized Migration

Transitioning from centralized identity systems to decentralized identities entails navigating several critical considerations. A successful transition to decentralized identities require a holistic approach that addresses interoperability challenges, promotes user understanding and adoption, and ensures compliance with evolving regulatory frameworks. The overall transition requires collaboration with various stakeholders, including industry partners, technology providers, and regulatory bodies.

First, interoperability poses a challenge as existing identity systems vary widely in technology and standards. To addresses this, it's crucial to adopt widely accepted standards such as those proposed by the Decentralized Identity Foundation and the World Wide Web Consortium (WWW). Implementing interoperability layers or gateways can facilitate communication between decentralized and centralized identity systems. Collaboration with industry stakeholders is essential to establish common protocols and practices, fostering a more cohesive and interconnected identity landscape.

Second, user adoption is pivotal for the success of the decentralized identity. Many users may be unfamiliar with the concept and may exhibit resistance to change. Robust education and awareness campaigns are necessary to inform users about the benefits, such as enhanced privacy and security and personal control over identity information. Ensuring user-friendly interfaces and experiences that simplify the management of DIDs and verifiable credentials can contribute to a smoother transition. Additionally, incentive programs or rewards may encourage early adoption, while showcasing the advantages of the new decentralized identity system.

Third, regulatory compliance is a complex challenge given the evolving nature of regulatory frameworks and data privacy laws. Proactive monitoring of regulatory changes and engagement with relevant authorities are necessary to ensure compliance. Designing decentralized identity systems with privacy and data protection principles in mind and aligning with regulations such as the EU's GDPR, India's DPDP Act 2023, or other regional protection laws are both crucial. Providing users with granular control over the data and incorporating consent management features are key components to meet regulatory requirements.

Beyond the Like Button: The Decentralized Social Experience

Social media is undergoing a transformative shift with the rise of decentralized platforms, signaling a departure from the centralized models that have defined our online interactions for years. Dominated by a few major players, traditional social media platforms have facilitated global connections that have concurrently sparked concerns over issues such as data privacy, user anatomy, and the commodification of user attention. In response to these challenges, a new era of decentralized social networks is emerging, driven by commitment to user-centricity and privacy preservation. These innovative platforms seek to revolutionize the social media experience by introducing new features that empower users and cultivate more meaningful connections.

Decentralized social networks are breaking away from the like-driven, dopamine-fueled approach of traditional platforms and introducing features that promote genuine engagement and meaningful interactions.

Decentralized Ownership and Governance

Unlike traditional platforms where decision-making is centralized, the decentralized network empowers users with a direct say in the platform governance. The user-centric approach ensures that the community interest and values are integral to the network's development. Through mechanisms such as voting on platform updates, content policies, and other crucial decisions, users actively participate in shaping the trajectory of the social network. The decentralized ownership and governance mark a departure from top-down control, placing the power of decision-making firmly in the hands of the community.

Content Ownership and Control

Decentralized social networks are a fundamental shift in the dynamics of content ownership and control, placing users at the forefront of these aspects. Unlike traditional platforms where content often becomes the property of the platform itself, decentralized networks prioritize user ownership. This means you can retain control over your content, from posts and media to other contributions. The significance of this lies not only in safeguarding intellectual property but also in empowering you to monetize your content directly.

Community-Driven Content Curation

The community-driven content curation is a feature of decentralized social networks, departing from the algorithm-driven approaches in traditional platforms. In the decentralized network, communities play a pivotal role in shaping the content landscape. Users within specific communities have the agency to curate and surface content that is deemed relevant and valuable and aligned with the interest of the members of the community. By enabling you to actively contribute to the content curation processes, decentralized social networks foster a more personalized and emerging user experience. This model not only mitigates algorithmic biases but also cultivates a sense of shared identity and purpose within communities.

Tokenized Rewards and Incentives

Decentralized social networks introduce a way to acknowledge and encourage meaningful contributions by users. In decentralized social networks, you have the opportunity to earn tokens as a form of recognition for the active participation in and valuable contributions to the platform. The tokens earned by you can hold intrinsic value within the network's ecosystem. You can utilize these tokens for various purposes, such as accessing premium features, trading with external cryptocurrencies, and so on.

Data Privacy and Security

Privacy and security are paramount considerations in decentralized social networks. In contrast to centralized models where your data is typically stored on servers controlled by a single entity, decentralized networks distribute and manage user data across decentralized infrastructure. Blockchain's cryptographic principles enhance the security of your data by ensuring that information is stored in a tamper-resistant and transparent manner. The decentralized nature of data storage reduces the risk of large-scale data breaches that are often associated with centralized platforms. Since there is no central repository for hackers to target, the impacts of security breaches are mitigated.

Various innovative features will evolve to empower users and foster meaningful connections. Decentralized social networks have the potential to transform the social media landscape for the better.

Future Trends and Outlook

The future of social media is on the brink of revolutionary transformation, fueled by the ascent of decentralized technologies and an escalating desire for platforms that prioritize user-centricity and privacy. Decentralized identities are expected to play a pivotal role in shaping this evolution. Anticipated developments include the refinement and widespread adoption of standardized protocols, leading to seamless interoperability and user-friendly decentralized identity solutions. As users increasingly seek alternatives that grant them greater control over their personal information, decentralized social networks are likely to gain prominence. These networks, underpinned by blockchain and cryptographic principles, promise enhanced privacy and security measures. Users retaining ownership of their data and being able to monetize their contributions through tokenized incentives will redefine the traditional social media landscape. Niche, community-centric platforms could flourish, offering specialized spaces for authentic interactions. Regulatory frameworks are likely to evolve to address the unique challenges and opportunities posed by decentralized social media platforms.

As decentralized identities become more prevalent, they are likely to unlock new social media use cases. These use cases are related to decentralized content creation, community governance structure, data-driven social impact initiatives, etc.

Case Studies

The concept of decentralized identity is still in its early stages of development, but there are a few real-world examples where users are using these platforms.

- **LBRY:** This is a decentralized social network platform that uses blockchain technology to store and manage your data. This means that you have complete control over your data and can choose whom to share your data with. LBRY also uses a cryptocurrency called LBC to reward you for creating and sharing content.

- **Brave:** Brave is a decentralized web browser that has built-in support for DID. This means you can create and manage your DIDs without having to use a separate application. Brave also has a built-in cryptocurrency wallet that allows you to tip content creators directly.

There are many upcoming social media platforms, but they are still in the early stages.[2]

Summary

This chapter started by outlining the current state and significance of social media in our lives and then traced the evolution from early digital communication to today's diverse social media landscape. The next section delved into the different types of social networks, comparing their structures. The chapter covered platforms that distribute control across multiple nodes and discussed their advantages and nuances.

---

[2] https://blocksurvey.io/web3-guides/decentralized-social-media-platforms

It also discussed how decentralized identities can be integrated into social networks, enhancing user privacy and control. The chapter gave an architectural overview of decentralized social networks and discussed the difficulties faced in creating and maintaining decentralized networks and their broader implications. It also covered how you can transition from centralized to decentralized platforms, considering user behavior and technological requirements. In a nutshell, this chapter provided a comprehensive overview of decentralized social media, from its conceptual foundations to its potential future trajectory.

CHAPTER 8

Health Care and Financial Systems with Decentralized Identity

This chapter introduces the transformative impact that decentralized identifiers (DIDs) could have on the healthcare and financial sectors. It outlines how DIDs will empower individuals and give them control over their personal data, enhancing privacy and security.

This chapter also outlines the challenges of adopting DIDs, including the need for regulatory compliance and system interoperability. This sets the stage for a deeper exploration of using DIDs to modernize these critical sectors.

Finally, this chapter details how DIDs is being implemented in various use cases.

Introduction

The digital era has brought significant advancements in how we manage and protect our personal details, particularly in critical sectors like finance and healthcare.

In the health sector, how we manage patient data, including personal health records, is a subject of paramount importance. Traditional systems, largely centralized, often face challenges in ensuring data security, patient privacy, and seamless information sharing between different hospitals and insurance companies. Decentralized identities offer a transformative solution, providing patients with unprecedented control over their personal health information. This approach not only enhances privacy and security but also facilitates interoperability among various healthcare providers, thereby improving the overall quality and efficiency of healthcare delivery.

© Shivakumar R. Goniwada 2024
S. R. Goniwada, *Introduction to One Digital Identity*, https://doi.org/10.1007/979-8-8688-0255-3_8

Similarly, in the financial services sector, including banking, insurance, investments, payments, and transfers, the need of robust identity verification and fraud prevention mechanism has never been greater. The rise of digital banking and online financial transactions demands a system that can reliably authenticate identities while ensuring user privacy. Decentralized identities address these needs by allowing consumers to manage and share their financial credentials securely and conveniently. They not only streamline the process of identity verification but also significantly reduce the risk of identity theft and financial fraud.

Implementing DIDs in these sectors is not without its challenges, including technological issues, regulatory compliance, and acceptance among stakeholders. However, the potential benefits, including enhanced data security, improved user experience, and greater operational efficiency, make this an exciting area to explore.

Redefining Healthcare: A Decentralized Approach

The current healthcare landscape, characterized by its complexity and the fragmentation of patient data across various providers and systems, presents considerable challenges in patient data management, access, and security. In this environment, DID technology emerges as a transformative solution with the potential to overhaul how health data is handled. DIDs can empower patients with unprecedented control over their health information, breaking down the silos that currently hinder efficient data management in healthcare.

DIDs allow patients to have a singular, secure digital identity that links to their health records, regardless of where the records are kept. This unified approach contrasts sharply with the existing system, where patient data is scattered across multiple healthcare providers and systems, making it challenging to access and share information efficiently. With DIDs, the patients can grant or revoke access to their health records as needed, facilitating seamless sharing among healthcare providers.

With the standard being created by the W3C, a DID can address the interoperability issue in healthcare. By providing a standard format for identities and data access, DIDs enable different healthcare systems and providers to communicate and share data more effectively. This interoperability is crucial for providing comprehensive and coordinated care, especially for patients with complex medical history who see multiple providers.

HIPPA and DIDs

DIDs can be particularly beneficial in the context of HIPAA, which sets standards for the protection of sensitive patient health information in the United States. By leveraging DIDs, healthcare organizations can enhance the privacy and security of patient data. For example, a patient's DID could serve as a unique secure identifier in the healthcare system, linked to their medical records. Unlike traditional identifiers, a DID is controlled by the individual identifiers, giving patients greater control over who accesses their health information.

In real-world scenarios, when a patient visits a healthcare provider, they could grant temporary access to their medical records through their DID, without needing to expose their personal information like their Social Security number (SSN). This method not only simplifies the verification process but also reduces the risk of data breaches, as DIDs can be designed to share only the necessary information while keeping the rest of information encrypted and secured.

Additionally, in research or third-party data sharing, DIDs can help de-identify the data, thereby maintaining compliance with HIPAA regulations about patient privacy. The use of DIDs aligns with HIPAA's goals of safeguarding patient privacy while ensuring that necessary health information is accessible to authorized parties, taking a step forward toward secure and patient-centric health information.

Patient Identification and Authentication

In the healthcare sector, patient identification and authentication are critical components that ensure the right patient receives the right treatment and that their medical records are accurately maintained. However, in traditional methods, multiple usernames and passwords often lead to complication and security risks.

With DIDs, each patient is assigned a unique digital identity that is used to access their health records and authenticate themselves across various healthcare platforms. This system eliminates the need for multiple usernames and passwords, which are not only cumbersome for patients to manage but also pose a significant security risk due to theft or loss. DIDs use the advanced cryptographic techniques to ensure that the patient's identity is secure and cannot be tampered with or forged.

Implementing DIDs in patient identification and authentication would involve patients creating their digital identity, which is then securely linked to their medical history and personal health records. When a hospital or doctor needs to access these records, the users authenticate themselves for the medical services by using the DID. Patients can decide which parts of their medical records can be accessed by whom, thus maintaining confidentiality and complying with privacy regulations like HIPAA.

Medical Record Management

Integrating DIDs into medical record management significantly empowers patients, providing them with unparalleled control and ease in managing health records. In this system, patients link their medical records to their personal DIDs. This approach transforms a traditional medical record-keeping system into a more patient-centric approach.

With the medical record tied to a DID, patients gain direct control over who can access their health information. The patients can seamlessly share their records with authorized healthcare providers as needed. For instance, when you are visiting a new specialist or the emergency room, you can grant immediate access to your comprehensive medical history, including past diagnosis, treatments, and test results, all through the DID. This access can be as broad or as restricted as you desire, ensuring privacy and consent are always at the forefront.

The benefits of this system extend beyond just patient control. For healthcare providers, this means access to a more complete and accurate medical history of the patient, leading to better informed decision-making and improved patient care.

For interoperability challenges between multiple healthcare systems and providers, the W3C is working on creating a standardized protocol that can bridge the gap between disparate healthcare systems.

Clinical Trials and Research

Using DIDs in clinical trials and research offers a solution that balances the need for comprehensive data access with the necessity of maintaining patient privacy. In clinical trials, sensitive patient data forms the backbone of the research. In the traditional model, the data is often challenged by privacy concerns and security risks. DIDs provide a solution to address these challenges effectively.

In the framework of DIDs for clinical trials, each patient is assigned a unique DID, a secure digital identity that is linked to their personal health data relevant to the study. This setup allows patients to have granular control over their data, as they can selectively grant or revoke access to specific portions of their health information to researchers or institutions involved in the trial. This mechanism not only enhances the security of the data but also places the power of consent firmly in the hands of the patient, ensuring that their privacy is respected and maintained throughout the research process.

Furthermore, DIDs facilitate the anonymization or pseudonymization of patient data when shared for research purposes, enabling researchers to access necessary information while safeguarding patient identity. This is crucial in adhering to ethical standards and regulatory compliance, such as GDPR, DPDP, HIPAA, and NIST, which mandate the protection of personal data in research environments.

From the perspective of researchers and clinical trial managers, DIDs offer a streamlined and efficient way to collect, manage, and share patient data. The uniformity and interoperability of DIDs simplify the complexities involved in handling data from diverse sources, making it easier to aggregate and analyze information from various participants. This efficiency is particularly beneficial in large-scale, multicenter trials where data consistency and integrity are paramount.

Insurance Claim Processing

DIDs can improve the insurance claim process by facilitating a secure, efficient, and verifiable exchange of data between healthcare providers and insurance companies. Traditionally, insurance claims processing is a tedious process that is prone to delays, errors, and fraud. DIDs offer a digital solution to these issues by establishing a secure and immutable identity for each patient that is linked to their insurance and health data.

When a patient receives a healthcare service, their healthcare provider can access the necessary information such as patient identity, treatment details, and billing information through the DID. The data that is securely linked to the DID is then transmitted to the insurance company for processing. Using DIDs ensures that the data exchanged is accurate, is up-to-date, and comes from a verified source, thereby significantly reducing the risk of errors and fraudulent claims.

For insurance companies, this translates to a more streamlined and efficient claims processing workflow. Immediate access to verified data reduces the need for manual verification and back-and-forth communication with healthcare providers, speeding up the claim's approval process. Additionally, the reduced risk of fraudulent claims and errors leads to cost savings for the insurers.

Telehealth and Remote Patient Monitoring

The integration of DIDs into telehealth and remote patient monitoring systems presents an implementable solution to the challenges of secure and compliant data sharing in vital healthcare services. With the rapid expansion of telehealth and growing reliance on remote monitoring especially in developing countries for patient care, ensuring the security and privacy of patient data is paramount. DIDs offer trustworthiness to digital healthcare services.

In a telehealth context, a DID can be used to create secure and verifiable digital identities for both patients and healthcare providers. When a patient engages in a telehealth consultation or participates in a remote patient monitoring program, their unique DID serves as a secure access point to their medical history and personal health information. This identity can be authenticated by the healthcare provider, ensuring that they are accessing the correct patient's details. Likewise, patients can verify the identity of healthcare providers, enhancing trust in the digital healthcare relationship.

In remote patient monitoring, where continuous data collection and sharing are essential, DIDs facilitate the secure transmission of health data from patients to healthcare providers. Devices used in remote monitoring can be linked to the patient's DID, ensuring that the data they collect is securely associated with the correct patient and is readily accessible by authorized healthcare professionals. This not only streamlines the monitoring process but also ensures that the data is accurate, up-to-date, and secure.

Moreover, the use of DIDs in telehealth and remote patient monitoring enables a more personalized and efficient healthcare experience. Healthcare providers can access a comprehensive, real-time view of the patient's health status, leading to better informed clinical decisions and more tailored treatment plans.

Challenges and Considerations

Implementing DIDs in healthcare must align with evolving data privacy regulations and healthcare compliance standards, a task that is both crucial and complex. Regulatory compliance is a key consideration, as DIDs handle sensitive personal information, particularly in healthcare where patient data is subject to stringent privacy laws and ethical considerations.

First, DIDs must comply with global data protection regulations such as GDPR in Europe, the DPDP Act in India, HIPAA in the United States, and other regional laws.

These regulations mandate strict guidelines for how personal data is collected, stored, processed, and shared. DIDs with their decentralized nature offer a framework where data control lies with the individual, aligning with the principle of data minimization and user consent to these regulations.

However, the challenges lie in ensuring that the DID infrastructure consistently adheres to these regulations, which can vary significantly across different jurisdictions. This requires DID systems to be flexible and adaptable to meet diverse regulatory requirements, including providing clear mechanisms for user consent, data access rights, and the right to be forgotten.

In healthcare, compliance with standards like HIPAA also means ensuring that DIDs are implemented in a way that safeguards protected health information (PHI). This involves encrypting PHI, ensuring secure data transmission, and implementing robust access controls. DIDs must ensure that only authorized individuals can access or share patient data and that there is a clear audit trail of all such interactions.

Furthermore, DIDs must be designed to support interoperability with existing healthcare IT systems, many of which are subject to their own regulatory compliance requirements. Seamless integration without compromising compliance is a critical aspect of DID implementation in healthcare.

To address these challenges, ongoing collaboration between technology developers, regulatory bodies, and industry stakeholders is essential. This collaboration can help in establishing clear guidelines and standards for DID implementation that are in harmony with existing laws and regulations.

Decentralized Identity and Its Relevance in Financial Services

Decentralized identities (DIDs) represent a paradigm shift in how customer identities are managed, verified, and utilized, addressing several longstanding challenges faced by the industry. At the core of the DID appeal is the enhanced security and reduced fraud risk. Traditional financial systems, with centralized repositories of personal data, are prone to large-scale data breaches. DID mitigates this by decentralizing the control of identity data, significantly lowering the chances of such breaches and consequently reducing identity theft and fraud.

Moreover, DID streamlines the customer onboarding processes, particularly the know-your-customer (KYC) procedures. Currently, KYC is a repetitive and paperwork-intensive process that can be a source of frustration for both customers and financial institutions. With DID, customers have a secure digital identity that can be used across various platforms, eliminating the need for repeated verification. This not only enhances the customer experience by making processes faster and more user-friendly but also significantly reduces the administrative and operational burdens on financial institutions.

Additionally, DIDs align closely with the growing emphasis on privacy and data sovereignty. In traditional systems, customers often relinquish control of their personal data to financial institutions. DIDs, on the other hand, empower customers to maintain control over their personal information, sharing only what is necessary for specific transactions. This approach respects and upholds individual privacy, a factor increasingly valued in the digital age.

Furthermore, compared to traditional identity systems, DIDs offer greater interoperability and efficiency. Traditional systems often operate in silos, with each institution maintaining its own customer identity records. This lack of interoperability can lead to inefficiencies and redundancies. A DID, by its nature, promotes a more interconnected system where identity data can be securely and efficiently shared across institutions, with the customer's consent, enhancing the overall functionality and user experience of financial services.

Streamlining KYC and the Compliance Process

The integration of DID in the KYC process marks a significant advancement in streamlining identity verification in financial services. KYC, a mandatory compliance procedure for financial institutions, involves verifying the identity of the clients to prevent fraud and money laundering.

As shown in Figure 8-1, a DID offers a more efficient alternative by enabling a digital, reusable identity. In this example, Nikki can store her government-issued identity information on a secure, decentralized platform. When financial institutions ask Nikki to update the KYC process, she can provide access to her verified identity data, thus eliminating the need for repeated verification. This not only speeds up the onboarding process but also enhances the customer experience by making it more seamless and less intrusive.

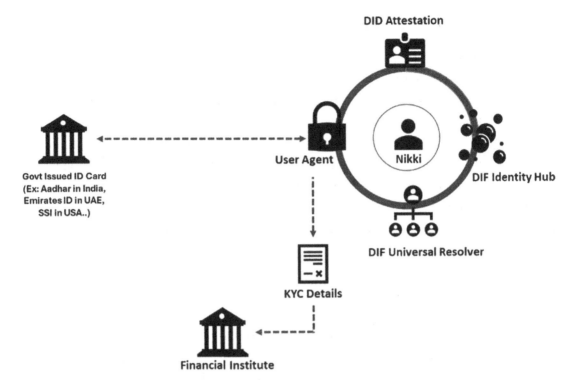

Figure 8-1. *KYC with a financial institute*

Electronic Identification, Authentication and trust Services (eIDAS) is a key element in the European Union's strategy to enhance trust in electronic transactions. The release of eIDAS 2.0 is expected to further strengthen the legal framework for electronic identification and trust services, including aspects related to a decentralized identity system. eIDAS 2.0 is set to mandate that businesses and government organizations within the EU accept verifiable decentralized identity credentials stored in digital wallets. This is a significant move for the technology as it places decentralized identities at the heart of Europe's digital infrastructure. KYC providers must prepare to integrate with this framework to comply with these new regulations, signaling a major shift in how identity verification processes will be conducted in the future in the EU.

Enhancing Security and Privacy with DID

DIDs enable financial institutions to verify user identities more securely. During crucial processes such as onboarding, authentication, and transactions, DIDs can be used to confirm the identity of users with greater accuracy. It will therefore also cut down on identity theft and fraud.

Identity Theft and Fraud with DID

Using DIDs for identity theft and fraud detection in financial systems provides a robust and innovative approach. DIDs serve as unique and verifiable identifiers for individuals, which is a departure from traditional centralized identity systems that are often susceptible to data breaches and manipulative attacks. This decentralized model inherently bolsters security and deters identity-related fraud in several ways.

Unlike centralized identity databases, DIDs are stored on a decentralized ledger, such as a blockchain. This means there is no single point of failure where the identity data can be compromised. Each DID is independently verifiable without needing to access a central database, making it much harder for attackers to steal or forge identities. One of the main principles of DIDs is "share what you need to share," so users can provide limited information necessary for a transaction, reducing the exposure of their full identity profile.

To detect fraud, the financial systems can integrate DIDs into their existing fraud detection systems. For example, transaction monitoring systems can use the unforgeable nature of DIDs to verify the identity of parties in real time, reducing the likelihood of fraudulent transactions. By combining DID-based verification with machine learning and behavioral analytics, financial transactions systems can detect unusual patterns indicative of fraud. Since DIDs provide a consistent and tamper-evident identity trail, it becomes easier to spot deviations from normal user behavior.

Customer Onboarding with DID

DIDs can be used to onboard customers too. When a new customer creates an account with a financial institution, the institution can be assigned a unique DID. This DID is the digital representation of their identity, securely linked to the verified personal information. The process involves validating the user's identity documents and biometric data, which is then cryptographically associated with their DID. For each transaction or login attempt, the financial institution can request that the user provide cryptographic proof that they control the DID. This proof can be a digital signature or a token generated by the user's device, linked to the DID. This method ensures that the person accessing the service or initiating the transaction is the legitimate owner of the DID, thereby preventing impersonation.

Open Banking and Decentralized Identity

Open banking and DIDs are reshaping the financial sector by enhancing how financial data is shared and managed. This convergence is pivotal in fostering a more secure, efficient, and user-centric financial ecosystem.

Open banking, a practice that allows third-party providers (TPPs) to access financial data through APIs with customer consent, is revolutionizing traditional banking models. It enables a more competitive environment where users benefit from personalized financial services, such as budgeting tools, investment advice, and loan offers. However, the success of open banking hinges on robust security and user trust, which is where DIDs can help.

When integrated with open banking, DIDs offer a robust framework for secure data sharing. Users can utilize their DIDs to authenticate themselves when accessing services offered by TPPs. This process not only streamlines user verification, eliminating the need for multiple passwords and verification steps, but also ensures that personal and financial data is shared only with explicit user consent. Moreover, DIDs can store user consent in a tamper-evident way, adding an extra layer of security and accountability.

The synergy between open banking and DID also fosters innovation in the financial sector. With secure and efficient data sharing mechanisms, financial institutions and TPPs can develop more sophisticated and tailored financial products and services.

Simplified Account Switching with DID

Simplified account switching, facilitated by DIDs, represents a significant leap forward in banking convenience and efficiency. In this scenario, switching from one bank to another becomes a seamless process, primarily driven by the capabilities of DIDs. Typically, changing bank accounts is a cumbersome process, involving extensive paperwork, multiple identity verification, and considerable time. However, with DIDs, the need for these traditional procedures is substantially reduced.

When you decide to switch a bank account, you simply update your DID with the new financial provider. The DID, being a secure and portable digital identity, contains all the necessary verified personal and financial information of the user. This data is already authenticated and stored in a decentralized manner, making it accessible and easily verifiable by the new bank. The new bank can then quickly and securely confirm your identity and associated details without the need for additional paperwork or manual verification processes.

This system not only accelerates the account switching process but also enhances security and reduces the risk of errors associated with manual data entry. The customer experiences a smooth transition, free from the usual administrative burdens and delays. Additionally, since DIDs are controlled by the user, they ensure that personal data is shared on a consent basis, adhering to privacy standards and giving customers greater control over information.

Streamlined Loan Applications with DIDs

Streamlined loan applications facilitated by DIDs represent a significant enhancement in the lending process, offering a more efficient, secure, and user-friendly approach. In a traditional loan application process, applications are required to provide extensive documentation to prove the customer's identity and income, which can be a time-consuming process. By using DIDs, this scenario changes dramatically.

DIDs enable loan applications to be automatically filled in with verified income and identity information. Since a DID is a secure digital identity that is controlled and managed by the user, it stores verified personal data, including financial details and identity credentials. When you apply for a loan, the financial institution can request access to specific information from your DID. With your consent, the relevant data, such as proof of income, employment history, and identity verification, can be securely and instantly transferred to the loan application.

This process significantly reduces the friction typically associated with loan applications. Applications no longer need to manually gather and submit multiple documents; instead, your DID provides a reliable and efficient means of sharing verified information. For lenders, this means quicker access to accurate and authenticated data, allowing for a more streamlined and faster vetting process. It also reduces the risk of fraudulent applications, as the information within a DID is tamper-evident and more reliable than traditional paper or manually submitted digital documents.

Cross-Border Transactions with DIDs

Cross-border transactions, critical to the global economy, often face challenges such as inefficiency and a lack of transparency, which DIDs are uniquely positioned to address and potentially revolutionize. In the realms of international trade, remittance, and investments, the seamless and secure flow of transactions across borders is paramount. DIDs provide a secure, verifiable, and decentralized digital identity for each participant in a transaction.

The primary advantage of DIDs in cross-border transactions is reduced friction and inefficiency. Traditional methods often involve cumbersome verification processes, with varying standards and practices across different countries. DIDs, however, allow for swift and uniform identity verification, streamlining the process significantly. This uniformity is especially beneficial in adhering to diverse regulatory environments, simplifying compliance with international standards like Anti-Money Laundering (AML) and KYC regulations.

Moreover, DIDs enhance transparency in cross-border transactions. In a landscape where transparency is often compromised because of the involvement of multiple intermediaries, DIDs maintain clear and traceability identity records. This traceability is crucial in reducing fraud and ensuring the legitimacy of all parties involved. By providing a decentralized approach to identity, DIDs ensure that no single entity controls the verification process, thereby reducing the risk of manipulation and increasing the overall integrity of transactions.

Additionally, the use of DIDs in cross-border transactions can lead to significant cost reductions. By eliminating redundant identity verification processes and reducing the reliance on intermediaries, transactions become more direct and less costly. This aspect is particularly beneficial for remittance, where reducing transaction fees is a long-standing goal.

Payments with Digital Wallets

Digital wallets, also known as e-wallets, allow individuals to make electronic payment transactions. These transactions can include purchasing items online with an electronic device such as a phone. Essentially, digital wallets can securely store a user's payment information and passwords.

Using DIDs with digital wallets heralds a new era in the domain of cross-border payments, characterized by increased speed and enhanced security. This approach significantly deviates from the traditional reliance on financial intermediaries, offering a more direct and efficient payment mechanism. In this mode, the DIDs are linked to individual digital wallets, creating a unique and secure identity for each user.

Using DIDs in conjunction with digital wallets for cross-border payments facilitates instantaneous transactions. Traditional international payments can be time-consuming, often taking days to process due to the involvement of multiple intermediaries and the need to navigate various national banking systems. However, with DIDs, the process is streamlined as the payment is transferred directly from one digital wallet to another, bypassing conventional banking channels. Moreover, using DIDs ensures that each transaction is securely tied to the identity of the sender and the receiver, thereby enhancing trust and transparency in the process.

Challenges to Adoption of DIDs in Financial Services

While DIDs hold immense promise for the financial sector, their widespread adoption faces several significant challenges.

Lack of Standardization and Interoperability

The absence of universally agreed-upon technical standards for DIDs leads to difficulties in ensuring seamless interaction between various DID systems and financial platforms. The lack of standardization results in isolated systems or silos, where DIDs implemented by one institution or in one country might not be compatible or recognizable by another. To address this issue, the W3C is working on creating a standardized protocol.[1]

Resistance to Change

Using DIDs in the financial sector faces considerable resistance from users of the traditional approach. These entities often view disruptive technologies like DIDs with apprehension, perceiving them as potential threats to the existing infrastructure, regulatory compliance frameworks, and so on. This wariness is compounded by the significant investment that these institutions have already made in the current systems, making them reluctant to adopt new, untested technologies.

To overcome this resistance, it is crucial to demonstrate the tangible benefits of DIDs by showcasing the value proposition of DIDs in terms of cost savings, enhanced security features, and improved customer experience. Clear demonstration and pilot projects can illustrate how DIDs will streamline the identity verification process, reduce fraud, and

---

[1] https://www.w3.org/TR/did-core/

enhance data privacy, all of which are critical concerns for financial institutions. Another key aspect is to ensure that the transition to DIDs is seen not as a replacement of existing systems but as a complementary addition that can coexist and gradually integrate with traditional frameworks.

Technical Barriers from Implementation

The implementation of DIDs within existing financial systems poses a technical challenge. These challenges are multifaceted, including integrating new technologies into established systems, ensuring system security and scalability, and complying with evolving regulatory frameworks. The technical complexity of blockchain technology, which underpins many DID systems, requires specialized skills that may not be available in many financial institutions. Legacy systems, which are common in many financial institutions, often lack the flexibility or capability to easily integrate with APIs.

Integration Challenges

Integrating DIDs into an enterprise ecosystem presents several challenges. The following are the few:

- **Legacy systems:** Integrating DIDs into the financial sector presents notable challenges, particularly due to reliance on legacy systems. These existing systems in enterprises are often deeply entrenched, designed decades ago, and are not inherently compatible with new technologies like the blockchain that underpins DIDs. Upgrading from a legacy system to one that supports DIDs involves not just technical changes but also a shift in the operational and business model.

- **Compatibility concerns:** This is a significant hurdle in integrating DIDs within the financial sector, primarily due to the existence of various protocols and standards. Each of these protocols has its own unique features and methods of operation, which can lead to interoperability issues when trying to integrate with the ecosystem.

Security and Scalability

Security and scalability are critical considerations in the implementation of DIDs, especially given their potential use in sensitive areas such as finance and personal identity management.

- **Blockchain scalability:** Scalability is a significant concern, especially in high-volume financial transactions. The blockchain faces a limitation in handling a large number of transactions efficiently. Most blockchain technologies have a finite capacity for processing transactions, leading to potential bottlenecks when the transaction volume is very high. This can result in slower transaction processing times and higher costs, as seen in networks like Bitcoin and Ethereum.

- **Regulatory compliance:** This presents a significant challenge when implementing DIDs within financial institutions, largely due to the evolving and often uncertain regulatory landscape for digital identities. Financial institutions must navigate a complex array of regulations that vary by jurisdiction and are frequently in flux as government and regulatory bodies attempt to keep pace with technological advancements, ensuring DID systems comply with these regulations, including those pertaining to data privacy, security, AML, and KYC requirements. Noncompliance not only poses legal risks but can also result in significant financial penalties and reputational damage.

Technological Expertise

The successful management of DIDs demands specialized skills in blockchain technology, cryptography, and related fields, which poses a significant challenge due to the existing skills gap in the workforce. As DIDs are based on relatively new and complex technologies, finding skilled professionals who possess the necessary experience can be difficult. This technology not only requires a deep understanding of the technical aspects of blockchain and cryptography but also requires awareness of security privacy and regulations. The skills gap can lead to delays in project timelines, increased costs due to the premium on specialized knowledge, and potential risk associated with improper implementation. To bridge this gap, enterprises need to invest in training programs and partner with educational institutions to train the professionals.

Examples of DIDs in Financial Institutions

DIDs are increasingly being explored and implemented by major financial institutions such as Mastercard, HSBC, and Bitbond.

Mastercard

Mastercard's investment in decentralized identity solutions marks a significant step forward in the evolution of secure and user-controlled identity verification within the financial industry.[2]

In 2021, Mastercard collaborated with Idemia and Samsung to launch a biometric payment card equipped with decentralized identity features. This initiative combines the security and convenience of biometric authentication with the principles of decentralized identity, offering a glimpse into the future of secure transactions. The biometric payment card integrates a user's biometric data, such as fingerprints, directly into the card. This feature adds a layer of security to transactions, as the card can be used only when matched with the owner's biometric data. The decentralized digital identity aspect comes into play by ensuring that the user's biometric data is stored securely on the card itself, rather than in a centralized database. This approach aligns with the core principles of decentralized identity systems.

HSBC

In 2020, HSBC collaborated with Canadian startup SecureKey technologies to streamline KYC processes using decentralized identity solutions. The initiative, leveraging a solution named Verified.me, is specifically aimed at enhancing the KYC procedures for HSBC's corporate customers. Verified.me is a decentralized platform that facilitates the secure and efficient sharing of KYC data between financial institutions and their customers. Verified.me handles the data; instead of storing customer data centrally, it allows the data

---

[2] http://innovationinsights.mastercard.com/building-a-new-infrastructure-for-digital-identity/p/1

to be managed and controlled by the customer themselves. The customer can decide when and with whom to share their information. For HSBC, this is a more streamlined and efficient way of conducting KYC checks.

Bitbond

Bitbond, a German online lending platform, has notably integrated decentralized identity solutions into its business to revolutionize the way borrowers are verified and loans are distributed. This approach uses decentralized identity technology and allows borrowers to securely prove their identity and creditworthiness directly on the platform.[3]

Summary

This chapter explored the transformative impact of DIDs in healthcare and financial systems, two sectors where security, privacy, and efficient data management are paramount.

In healthcare, DIDs offer a patient-centric approach to medical record management, enabling patients to control their health data securely. This technology facilitates seamless sharing of medical records among healthcare providers. DIDs also streamlines processes in telehealth and remote patient monitoring, providing secure and real-time patient data access to healthcare professionals. Additionally, DIDs enhance clinical trials and research by enabling secure, consensual data sharing while protecting patient anonymity. Crucially, the implementation of DIDs in healthcare must comply with stringent data privacy regulations such as HIPAA, GDPR, and the DPDP Act.

In the financial sector, DIDs can revolutionize identity verification, reducing fraud and simplifying processes such as onboarding, transaction processing, and open banking. They enable secure and efficient operations like KYC and cross-border transactions, where they address challenges of security, trust, and regulatory compliance.

This chapter underscored the potential of DIDs to enhance modernization, digitization, security, and user experience in the healthcare and financial sectors, while acknowledging the challenges and regulatory considerations that come with adopting this emerging technology.

---

[3] https://www.bitbond.com/

CHAPTER 9

Next Generation Digital Frontier

This chapter explores the evolving landscape of digital web technologies such as the metaverse, the Internet of Things (IoT), and Web 3.0 and how decentralized identities will affect them.

The chapter will answer the following questions:

- How will these technologies change the behavior of the Internet?

- What impact will these advancements have on data privacy, security, and digital ethics?

- How will decentralized identities (DIDs) empower these technologies to move in the right direction?

- How do Web 3.0 and DIDs complement each other?

This chapter provides insights into the opportunities and challenges that lie ahead in the next generation of the digital revolution.

Introduction to the Digital Frontier: Metaverse, IoT, and Web 3.0

The digital landscape is rapidly evolving, driven by groundbreaking technological advancements that are reshaping our world. At the forefront of this transformation are the metaverse, IoT, Web 3.0 and decentralized identities. Each of these domains represents a significant leap forward in how we interact with digital technology, offering new possibilities and challenges.

© Shivakumar R. Goniwada 2024
S. R. Goniwada, *Introduction to One Digital Identity*, https://doi.org/10.1007/979-8-8688-0255-3_9

The metaverse is an expansive virtual world that offers seamless integration with the physical world. It combines elements of virtual reality (VR), augmented reality (AR), and the Internet to create a space where users can interact with a computer-generated environment and each other in real time. This integration blurs the boundaries between the digital and physical realms, enabling an immersive experience that extends beyond traditional screen-based interactions. Users can socialize, play, work, and learn in the digital universe, often with enhanced realism. The metaverse also opens up possibilities for user-generated content, allowing individuals to create and modify their digital surroundings. Its potential extends across various industries, from education to entertainment, revolutionizing the way we engage with digital content.

IoT refers to a network of interconnected devices that are embedded with sensors, software, and other technologies to collect and exchange data with other devices and system over the Internet. This interconnectedness allows for a high level of automation and the creation of small networks. Devices in an IoT network can range from ordinary household items such as thermostats and refrigerators to sophisticated industrial tools. By collecting data from their environments, these devices can make intelligent decisions and carry out actions without human intervention, leading to increased efficiency, convenience, and energy savings. IoT is transforming various sectors, including home automation, healthcare, agriculture, and manufacturing, by enabling more responsive and data-driven approaches.

Web 3.0 represents a decentralized evolution of the Internet, built fundamentally on blockchain technology. This new iteration of the Web shifts away from the centralized structures of previous Internet generations, instead emphasizing user-centric data ownership and control. In Web 3.0, users have direct control over their data, as opposed to relying on large corporations that traditionally manage online information. This technology enables decentralized applications and smart contracts, allowing users to interact in a peer-to-peer fashion without intermediaries. Web 3.0 also integrates cryptocurrencies and digital assets, facilitating a new economic model within the digital space.

These technologies form a complex and synergistic ecosystem, rather than existing as isolated entities. The metaverse, envisioned as a vast, immersive virtual space, benefits immensely from the real-world data provided by IoT devices, enriching the virtual experience with elements from the physical world. This interaction enables more lifelike and interactive simulations and applications.

In parallel, Web 3.0's decentralized, blockchain-based infrastructure offers a fundamental layer for the metaverse, ensuring secure, transparent, and user-governed environments. This integration facilitates virtual economies, enabling users to have true ownership of digital assets. IoT, meanwhile, gains enhanced security and privacy through Web 3.0's decentralized networks, allowing for more secured data transfer and management, crucial for the functionality and reliability of IoT systems.

Related to all of these technologies is the concept of decentralized identity, which empowers users to control their personal and digital identities across platforms. This is crucial for maintaining privacy and security and for ensuring trust and personalization in digital interactions in the next generation of the Internet. Together, these technologies will create a more interconnected, efficient, and user-focused digital ecosystem, with each component enhancing the capabilities and possibilities of others.

The Convergence of the Metaverse and Decentralized Identities

In the growing realm of the metaverse, an immersive and interconnected virtual world, the management of identity will help shape its success and user experience. The metaverse promises a revolution in human interaction, offering a digital landscape where boundaries between the virtual and reality blur, allowing for unprecedented levels of engagement, collaboration, and creativity.

However, this virtual world's potential can only be fully realized with a robust and secure system for managing identity. This is where DIDs come into play as a transformative approach. Unlike traditional identity systems, DIDs are built on blockchain technology, providing users with self-sovereignty over their digital identities. This means individuals have complete control over their personal information, deciding how, when, and with whom to share the data. DIDs enable seamless and secure interactions and transactions, crucial for building an integrated and reliable virtual environment. With DIDs, users can navigate the metaverse with a consistent and verifiable identity across various platforms and experiences, ensuring a cohesive and personalized virtual journey.

Need of Digital Identities in the Metaverse

In the metaverse, the need for a robust identity system is crucial, mirroring the importance of identity in the physical world but with unique challenges and opportunities. Personalization is vital in the metaverse, as it allows experiences to be tailored to individual preferences and needs, enhancing user engagement and satisfaction. Trust and security are also crucial, because users engage in various interactions and transactions, so a secure identity system instills confidence and safety. Accountability is also essential, as it ensures users are responsible for their actions, fostering a respectful and law-abiding virtual community. Additionally, ownership and control over digital assets and personal data are critical, empowering users and safeguarding their digital autonomy.

Traditional online identity solutions, which are often centralized and managed by third-party platforms, are inadequate for the metaverse. These systems pose significant privacy and security risks and lack interoperability across different virtual environments, leading to fragmented experiences. The solution lies in DIDs, which offer a more secure, private, and user-controlled approach. Leveraging blockchain technology, DIDs enable users to own and manage their digital identities without relying on central authorities. Users can maintain a consistent identity and easily manage their digital assets and data across multiple virtual spaces.

Implementing DIDs in the Metaverse

Implementing DIDs in the metaverse is a multistep approach to ensure that users have secure, verifiable, and self-sovereign identities. The following tips will help you to implement and configure DIDs in the metaverse:

- **Adopt blockchain technology:** The foundation of DIDs is blockchain technology. Choose a suitable blockchain platform that meets the requirements of scalability, interoperability, and data privacy.

- **DID framework:** Use a DID framework that allows users to create and manage digital identities.

- **Interoperability:** One of the main challenges of both the metaverse and DIDs is interoperability across different platforms and virtual environments. As the W3C is developing standards and protocols, your environment must be designed to ensure that is compatible with various platforms, allowing users to maintain single identity.

- **Integrate verifiable credentials:** Incorporate verifiable credentials that allow users to prove aspects of their identity without revealing all the details.

- **User control and consent:** Empowers users with full control over their identity data. Implement consent mechanisms where users can decide what information to share, with whom, and under what circumstances.

- **Secure data storage:** Although the blockchain records transactions, personal data should not be directly stored on the blockchain due to privacy concerns. Instead, use secure, off-chain storage solutions that interact with the blockchain for verification purposes.

- **User experience:** Create intuitive and user-friendly interfaces that allow users to manage their DIDs easily. This can include digital wallets or other tools for managing identity credentials and permissions.

- **Legal and regulatory compliance:** The platform must ensure adhere to the legal and regulatory compliance requirements such as GDPR, DPDP, and so on. This could be challenging as each country has its own regulatory requirements.

These tips are mandatory to integrate DIDs in the metaverse, but don't create all the components from scratch; implement ready-to-use and proven software already available in cloud platforms.

Benefits of Decentralized Identities in the Metaverse

DIDs in the metaverse significantly enhance user experience and security. First, they bolster security and privacy. Since the data is not stored centrally, it is less vulnerable to breaches.

Interoperability is another key benefit of using decentralized identities in the metaverse. Decentralized identities enable users to seamlessly move and operate across different virtual worlds and platforms without the need for multiple, disjointed identities and credentials.

DIDs significantly empower users by placing them in full control of their digital personas. Users can manage their digital identities, assets, and experiences in the metaverse. The next section details a few applications in the metaverse where digital identities play a significant role. This level of control also encourages active participation and investment in the metaverse, as users will feel a strong sense of ownership and agency over their digital interactions.

Decentralized Identity Applications in Metaverse Applications

In the metaverse, DID technology can have far-reaching uses, significantly impacting how users interact, transact, and experience virtual environments. The following are some potential areas in the metaverse where DIDs can be used.

Login and Authentication

In the metaverse, where users navigate through multiple virtual environments and platforms, the existing login systems, requiring separate accounts and credentials for each platform, become cumbersome and pose security risks. Decentralized identities offer a transformative solution to this challenge. By implementing DID systems, users can log in with a single, portable identity credential that they control and manage, significantly streamlining the authentication process across various virtual environments.

Login becomes a seamless, one-click process. Users authenticate themselves through cryptographic methods such as biometrics to ensure a high level of security. This method also eliminates the need for users to remember multiple passwords or undergo repetitive registration processes for each new platform. This process also empowers users with greater control over their digital identities, fostering a more integrated and user-friendly virtual experience across diverse platforms and environments.

Digital Commerce

In digital commerce, DID plays a crucial role in enhancing transaction security and user experience in the metaverse. Virtual markets and stores in the metaverse, much like their real-world counterparts, require reliable methods of transactions and identity verification. DID enables this by allowing users to prove their identity during purchases without exposing sensitive personal data. This is achieved through the use of cryptographic techniques and blockchain technology, where a user's identity and transaction credentials are securely encrypted and verified without revealing underlying personal information.

For sellers, this system ensures the authenticity and accountability of their customers. They can verify that the person making the purchase is who they claim to be, significantly reducing the risk of fraud. On the buyer's side, the use of DIDs in transactions means that they can shop with confidence, knowing that their personal and financial data is not being unnecessarily exposed or stored in a centralized database vulnerable to breaches.

Social Interactions and Networking

In the social landscape of the metaverse, DIDs transform how users engage in virtual social spaces, adding a layer of trust and authenticity to user interactions. In this digital environment, where social connections and networking form a significant part of the user experience, the ability to establish verifiable and secure profiles is crucial. DIDs facilitate this by enabling users to create digital identities that are not only unique and tamper-proof but also respect user privacy. The DID ensures consistent identity as users navigate through different virtual environments and communities within the metaverse.

The key to implementing DIDs in social interactions and networking within the metaverse lies in its integration across different platforms and communities. This requires a standardization of identity protocols to ensure interoperability, allowing users to maintain a consistent identity as they move across various virtual environments.

Virtual Asset Ownership and Transfer

Implementing DIDs for virtual asset ownership and transfer in the metaverse, particularly for nonfungible tokens (NFTs), involves a technical framework grounded in blockchain technology. In this system, each digital asset, be it virtual real estate, art, or collectibles, is represented as an NFT, which is essentially a unique digital token on the blockchain, ensuring its authenticity and single ownership. When a user acquires an NFT, their decentralized identity is securely associated with the token, creating an immutable record of ownership on the blockchain. This record provides a clear and indisputable proof of ownership, crucial in the metaverse's digital economy.

For the secure transfer of assets, smart contracts are employed. These are self-executing contracts with the terms of the agreement embedded in the code, and they automatically facilitate, verify, and enforce the negotiation performance of a contract. When a user decides to transfer an NFT, the smart contract executes the transfer once the agreed-upon conditions are met.

Integrating this system into the metaverse requires a seamless interface where users can easily manage their digital assets and identities. This includes intuitive platforms for buying and selling and transferring NFTs, along with robust security measures to protect against unauthorized access and fraud. Interoperability is the key, as assets might be used across various metaverse environments and need to be recognized and operable across the various virtual environments.

Challenges of Future Development

While DIDs bring numerous benefits to the metaverse, they also face significant challenges that must be addressed for their successful implementation and widespread adoption.

One of the primary challenges is the adoption and integration of decentralized identity solutions into existing virtual environments. They need seamless integration to the diverse platforms in the metaverse. This requires an extensive collaboration between various stakeholders including the technical team, the platform owner, and the metaverse platform.

Another challenge is the technical complexity of DID systems. The underlying blockchain technology and cryptographic process can be complex and difficult for the average user to understand and navigate. This complexity can act as a barrier to entry for many users who might be hesitant to adopt new technologies that they do not fully comprehend. To overcome this, there is a need for user-friendly interfaces and educational resources that simplify the complexities of decentralized identities for end users.

Innovations of Future Development

The future of identity in the metaverse, particularly DIDs, presents a landscape ripe for innovation and growth.

An emerging trend is the concept of multidimensional avatars, which will offer users unprecedented control over their virtual personas. These avatars can be intricately customized in appearance and behavior and can be linked to different DID profiles tailored for various contexts or environments within the metaverse. This flexibility allows users to navigate diverse virtual spaces with appropriate, context-specific identities, enhancing both personal expression and privacy.

Another trend is the establishment of on-chain reputation systems. Leveraging the immutable and transparent nature of blockchain technology, these systems will use verifiable credentials to establish and maintain a user's reputation across different platforms. Such a system ensures that the reputation, once earned, is recognizable, secure, and transferable, fostering trust and credibility within the metaverse community.

The concept of NFT interoperability will take the utility of NFTs beyond digital asset representation. NFTs begin to represent elements of a user's identity, including their achievements and reputation, allowing for the seamless transfer and recognition of these elements across various metaverse platforms. This interoperability will significantly improve the user experience.

The integration of DIDs with AI marks a significant advancement in the field of identity verification and security, offering an enhancement in how identities are verified and secured.

Initially, AI algorithms will take a deep dive into a plethora of data sources, including social media, public records, and transaction histories, to verify the authenticity of DID claims. This comprehensive analysis allows AI to uncover any discrepancies or warning signs that might indicate fraudulent activities, making it increasingly difficult for imposters to create fake identities or mimic legitimate users. Moving forward, AI will leverage its learning capabilities to recognize and respond to unusual behavior patterns in real time. It will meticulously examine any deviations from normal user activities, such as irregular login attempts or transactions, and promptly identify and alert on potential fraud, thereby preemptively mitigating possible financial or data breaches.

Further enhancing the system, AI will utilize machine learning to customize the identity verification process. It will adjust the complexity and nature of verification steps according to the specific risk profile associated with each transaction or identity claim, thereby balancing heightened security with an improved user experience for legitimate individuals. This personalized approach ensures that verification is both stringent and user-friendly.

However, the deployment of AI in conjunction with DIDs necessitates a careful consideration of ethical standards. It's imperative to maintain transparency regarding how data is utilized to secure explicit user consent for data processing and to implement strong security protocols to safeguard personal information so that users can trust the system.

The Convergence of IoT and Decentralized Identities

IoT represents a transformative leap in technology, connecting physical objects to the digital realm and significantly impacting various sectors. By integrating objects with Internet connectivity, IoT blurs the line between the physical and virtual worlds, offering remarkable capabilities in detection, identification, information processing, and connectivity. This technology plays a pivotal role in diverse fields, including healthcare, transportation, home appliance, agriculture, and urban infrastructure, making it a cornerstone of the fourth industrial revolution.

During the COVID-19 pandemic, IoT's value was particularly evident in the healthcare sector. It provided crucial tools for patient investigation and data aggregation, enabling healthcare providers to gather and analyze patient data efficiently. Remote monitoring became a game-changer, allowing medical professionals to track patients' health status in real time while minimizing physical contact. IoT devices were instrumental in measuring body temperature and complying with quarantines.

In transportation, IoT technologies facilitate improved guidance and control systems, enhancing safety and efficiency. The trade industry benefits from IoT through optimized supply chain management and inventory tracking. The industrial automation leverages IoT technologies in precision farming, enabling farmers to monitor and optimize crop growth and health through sensors and data analysis.

Also, IoT has a profound impact on urban infrastructure, contributing to the development of smart cities. The continued expansion of IoT applications reflects its versatility and potential to revolutionize various aspects daily life and industry.

Identity Challenges in the IoT System

The evolving interconnectedness of the world has created significant challenges in managing the relationship between IoT devices and their users. The challenges of interoperability, integration, and security have led to a growing recognition of the need for decentralized identities.

- **Interoperability:** This is a major hurdle due to the absence of uniform identity and access management (IAM) standards for IoT devices. Manufacturers often resort to proprietary methods for naming and identifying their devices, leading to the creation of isolated IoT application ecosystems. This fragmentation severely limits the ability of devices from different manufacturers to communicate and function cohesively. A decentralized identity approach can address this by establishing a unified, standardized method for device identification and interaction, breaking down barriers between disparate IoT systems.

- **Integration:** Challenges arise as IoT systems evolve through various stages of their life cycle. Traditional identity solutions struggle to adapt to these changes, making it difficult to integrate identity capabilities seamlessly into IoT devices' operational frameworks. DIDs offer greater flexibility and adaptability, enabling the easier integration of identity management features at any stage of an IoT device's life cycle. This flexibility ensures that identity capabilities can evolve alongside the devices they are designed to protect.

- **Security:** Even though current IoT solutions use the OAuth open standard for security, there is no standardized approach across different IoT platforms. The DID model can offer a more uniform and secure framework. By leveraging technologies such as the blockchain, decentralized identity solutions can provide a secure, tamper-proof system for managing identities across a wide range of devices.

The Need of a DID Solution in IoT Devices

The current landscape of IoT systems often relies on OAuth, a prevalent open standard for web-based process to manage authentication and authorization. OAuth's approach, known as IoT-OAuth in the context of IoT, typically involves centralized servers that manage access permissions by issuing tokens to authenticated users. These tokens serve as digital keys, granting user access to various IoT resources and services. This centralized model has proven effective in handling authentication and authorization efficiently, providing a streamlined and secure way to manage access rights across diverse IoT devices and platforms.

However, the centralized nature of OAuth presents inherent vulnerabilities and privacy concerns, primarily the risk of a single point of failure. If the centralized server is compromised, it can lead to significant security breaches, potentially affecting all connected devices and users. This vulnerability is particularly concerning in the IoT context, where the interconnected nature of devices can amplify the impact of such breaches.

Implementing DIDs in IoT Systems

As explained many times in earlier chapters, the DID-leveraging blockchain technology empowers individuals with control over their identities, in contrast to traditional client-server and trust agency models. Figure 9-1 illustrates a DID implementation in IoT devices. The different components of the proposed architecture interact to provide a secure and efficient system for managing access and identity in the IoT environment. The main components include users, IoT devices, blockchain, smart contracts, a DID resolver, and DID attestation.

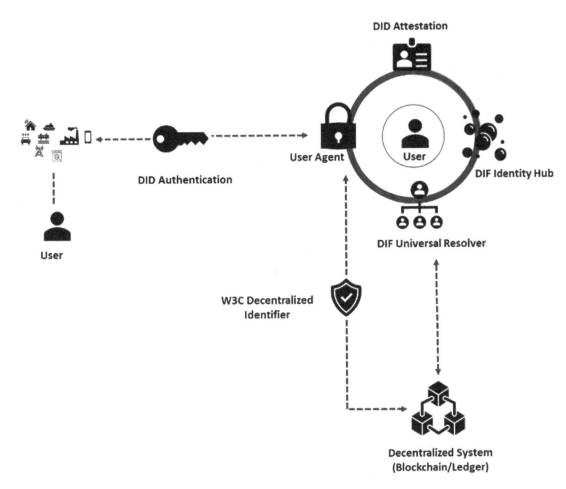

Figure 9-1. *DID in an IoT system*

Here's a breakdown of the components:

- **Users:** In this context, the users are individuals who want to register and access IoT devices and applications, such as e-health systems, smart watches, smart homes, autonomous vehicles, and so on. The user is the owner of the resources that the IoT devices aim to access. They have the authority to delegate access rights to their IoT devices, enabling these devices to use and manage the user's information on the user agent.

- **IoT devices:** These are the devices that a user wants to access. These devices, such as wearable technology like smart phones, self-driving cars, and smart home systems, are authorized by the user to access and manage information on their behalf. An IoT device acts as an intermediary, leveraging the user's delegated authority to interact with device agent.

- **Blockchain and smart contracts:** The blockchain nodes utilize smart contracts to authenticate and authorize users and IoT devices. Once users and IoT devices are verified through smart contracts, their transactions are recorded on the distributed ledger. The blockchain issues a token for access, which is also recorded on the ledger. The secure token key, requested by the DID identity hub, undergoes verification and recording, effectively serving as an authentication server.

- **DIF universal resolver:** This component is critical for locating, resolving, and retrieving a DID document that contains the authentication keys and methods for users and IoT devices. The DID resolver uses the DID to find the relevant document and delivers it to the blockchain, ensuring that the authentication information is up-to-date and accurate.

- **DIF identity hub:** The hub is responsible for storing and managing the user's resources. When an IoT device attempts to access these resources using tokens, the identity hub calls upon smart contracts on the blockchain to verify the integrity and ownership of these tokens. Once verified, the identity hub delivers the protected user resources to the IoT devices through a user agent.

Let's consider an example of our daily usage of smart watches and smart phones in an IoT context. In this setup, Nikki as a user connects her smart watch to her smart phone, establishing a link between the IoT device (her smart watch) and the client (her smart phone). The core of this system's security lies in the use of DIDs, which are authenticated through a blockchain network. This process involves both Nikki and her smart watch. Upon successful authentication, the blockchain records the authentication status, ensuring transparent and tamper-proof access. Following authentication, the DID issues a token to authenticate her smart watch. The token is essential as it authorizes the smart watch to access the user's sensitive biometric data stored on a DID attestation. This data can include various personal health metrics such as weight, height, heart rate, etc., that are monitored by smart watches.

The DID attestation, upon receiving a request for data access, performs a crucial verification process. It checks the token that the smart watch presents, which is provided and authenticated by the DID. This verification process is pivotal to ensure that the access request is legitimate and that the data is being shared with an authenticated and authorized device. Once the DID attestation confirms the legitimacy of the smart watch token, it proceeds to deliver the requested biometric data.

Challenges and Limitations

The integration of DIDs in IoT presents a promising avenue for enhancing security and privacy but faces significant challenges and limitations. A key technical challenge is the lack of standardization. Without universally accepted DID standards, there are compatibility issues across various platforms and devices, impeding interoperability. Additionally, many IoT devices are constrained in terms of processing power and storage, making it difficult to implement complex DID-based identity mechanisms. Developing lightweight yet secure cryptographic algorithms that suit these resource-limited devices is another ongoing challenge.

Managing the life cycle of DID keys, especially across various devices, is complex, necessitating secure storage and efficient distribution mechanisms. From a scalability and interoperability perspective, managing the identities of billions of connected devices, each with its own DID, is daunting. Efficient mechanisms are needed for scalable identity verification and resolution. Data exchange between devices with different DID implementations calls for robust data formats and protocols. Moreover, while decentralization offers enhanced security, it also presents challenges in network management and governance, demanding a balance between security and operational efficiency.

The adoption of DID also faces hurdles; there is a general lack of awareness about DIDs and their benefits, slowing adoption across the IoT ecosystem. Progress in establishing a universal DID standard has been slow, which discourages widespread implementation. The cost of integrating DID-based solutions, requiring additional infrastructure and development efforts, can be prohibitive for many businesses.

The Convergence of Web 3.0 and Decentralized Identities

Web 3.0 represents the envisioned evolution of the Internet, fundamentally shifting toward a decentralized architecture in contrast to the current Web 2.0 landscape. This new iteration is predicated on the principle of user empowerment and control over data, diverging from the centralized model where major platforms have data silos.

At its core, Web 3.0 leverages blockchain technology and decentralized ledger systems to facilitate peer-to-peer interactions, eliminating the need for central intermediaries. This decentralization ensures that users retain ownership and control over their data and digital identities, a stark contrast to Web 2.0, where large tech companies control user information.

Furthermore, Web 3.0 introduces the concept of a machine-readable web, enabled by smart contracts and AI, which allows for more intelligent, automated interaction between users and digital services. This shift not only promises enhanced privacy and security for users but also fosters a more open and interconnected digital ecosystem, where applications and services operate seamlessly across various platforms without the constraints imposed by centralized authorities. The vision of Web 3.0 is thus a more equitable and transparent Internet, where users have greater autonomy and the digital space becomes more democratically accessible.

Evolution from Web 2.0 to Web 3.0

The evolution of Web 2.0 to Web 3.0 represents a significant shift in how the Internet is structured and used. Web 2.0, which emerged in the early 2000s, marked a departure from the static, read-only websites of Web 1.0, introducing a new era characterized by user-generated content and interactivity. Platforms like social media sites and blogs became the new norm, empowering users to create, share, and interact with content. This era saw the rise of social networking services such as Facebook, Google, etc., which revolutionized how people connect and form online communities.

Another hallmark of Web 2.0 was the advent of dynamic web applications, which replaced the static websites of the earlier web era. These applications provided richer, more engaging user experiences and transformed the Web into an interactive platform rather than just an information repository.

Moreover, Web 2.0 was significantly marked by the rise of cloud computing. The shift to centralized services to host data and applications was a game-changer, offering unprecedented scalability and accessibility to users and businesses alike. Cloud services like Amazon Web Service (AWS), Azure, and Google Cloud emerged to provide robust and flexible computing resources over the Internet.

Web 2.0 brought forth significant concerns around data privacy, censorship, and interoperability, leading to the conceptualization of Web 3.0 as a solution.

- In Web 2.0, centralized platforms amassed vast quantities of user data, often with limited transparency or control for the users, raising serious data privacy concerns.

- These Web 2.0 platforms, due to their centralized nature, also possessed considerable power to censor content and control user behavior, leading to debates about freedom of expression and digital rights.

- Additionally, Web 2.0 was marked by limited interoperability, as data and functionality were typically confined within individual platforms. This siloing effect impeded collaboration and innovation, as sharing and integrating data across different ecosystems is challenging.

Web 3.0, in response, seeks to rectify these limitations.

- First, it advocates for decentralization by leveraging blockchain technology, which empowers users to own their data and participate in decision-making processes. This approach significantly reduces the dependency on centralized entities and platforms.

- Second, Web 3.0 places a strong emphasis on data ownership and privacy, giving users more control over their data, including how it is shared and utilized. This shift represents a move toward more transparent and user-centric data practices.

- Interoperability is another cornerstone of Web 3.0, with the ongoing development of open standards and protocols by W3C community, which facilitates seamless data exchange and collaboration across diverse platforms and applications. This interoperability not only enhances user experience but also foster innovation by allowing different systems to work together more efficiently.

- Another important concept in Web 3.0 is the semantic web, where data is machine-readable and can be processed by algorithms for more intelligent and personalized web experiences. This aspect of Web 3.0 enables a more intuitive and responsive digital environment, where information is not just accessible but also understandable by machines, paving the way for advanced applications like AI-driven personal assistants and sophisticated data analytics.

Core Technologies in Web 3.0

Web 3.0, the next iteration of the Internet, is built on a foundation of several transformative technologies. Each of the following plays a pivotal role in shaping its decentralized and intelligent ecosystem:

- **Blockchain:** This will be the main network for Web 3.0, providing a secure and transparent mechanism for recording transactions across a network of computers. It allows the creation of immutable records of transactions, fostering a new level of trust and transparency in digital interactions.

- **Decentralized applications (dApps):** Built on blockchain networks, dApps run autonomously without the need for central controlling entities. They often use smart contracts to automate processes and transactions, offering a new level of efficiency and security.

- **Tokenization:** This involves representing digital and physical assets as tokens on a blockchain, enabling new models of ownership and exchange. Tokenization can apply to a wide range of assets, from real estate to intellectual property, simplifying transactions and increasing liquidity in various markets.

- **Artificial intelligence (AI):** AI plays a key role in processing and analyzing the vast amounts of data generated in the Web 3.0 ecosystem.

- **IoT:** IoT is an essential component of Web 3.0, connecting physical objects to the Internet. This connectivity enables the collection and exchange of data from a myriad of devices, enriching the Web 3.0 landscape with real-world information and enabling new applications that blend the digital and physical worlds.

Integration of Web 3.0 with Decentralized Identities

The transition from Web 2.0 to Web 3.0 signifies a fundamental shift in the Internet's architecture, moving from a centralized one to a decentralized, user-centric model. This shift has profound implications for identity management online, a domain traditionally dominated by a centralized identity system.

In the Web 2.0 paradigm, identity verification is typically managed by central authorities or platforms, which store and control access to user data. DIDs are emblematic of the Web 3.0 ethos. DIDs represent a paradigm shift in how online identities are created, verified, and managed. Unlike the centralized model, DIDs empower users with direct control over their digital identities without relying on any central authority. This approach aligns with the core principles of Web 3.0 decentralization.

The change to Web 3.0 and decentralized identities is not just a technological upgrade but a fundamental rethinking of online interactions and data management. By leveraging blockchain technology and cryptography, Web 3.0 technologies are set to be the catalyst for a new era of online identity management.

Interoperability is a crucial advantage brought forth by decentralized identity solutions within the Web 3.0 framework. In the decentralized paradigm, identity systems are designed to work seamlessly across various networks and services, unlike the siloed and platform-specific identities prevalent in Web 2.0. This interoperability is made possible by leveraging open standards and protocols inherent in blockchain technology, which allows different systems and applications to communicate and recognize identities consistently and securely.

Moreover, interoperable decentralized identities facilitate a more fluid and integrated digital ecosystem. Users can interact with various applications, from financial services (DeFi) to social media platforms, using a single, secure digital identity. This system eliminates the need for intermediaries in identity verification.

DID Solutions

Several companies are creating Web 3.0 DID solutions to address the challenges posed by centralization, lack of user control, and security risk in digital identity management. Here are some examples:

- Spruce ID is working on a user agent that enables users to control their identities and data across different platforms securely. This approach is focused on creating interoperable solutions that work within the existing web infrastructure, aiming to make decentralized identity more accessible and user-friendly.

- Polygon ID is leveraging blockchain technology for its DID solution. By building on the Polygon network, known for its scalability and Ethereum compatibility, Polygon ID aims to provide a decentralized identity framework that can handle a high volume of transactions efficiently, making it suitable for large-scale applications.

- Microsoft also recognizes the need for a new approach to digital identity; the company's initiatives in the realm of decentralized identities are part of a broader commitment to building more secure and trustworthy digital ecosystems.

Challenges and Solutions

Web 3.0 and DIDs face a spectrum of challenges, encompassing technical integration difficulties, privacy and security concerns, and regulatory and ethical considerations.

One of the primary hurdles is integrating DIDs with existing digital ecosystems and ensuring interoperability across diverse platforms and blockchains. This requires not only technical know-how but also the development of universal standards and protocols to enable seamless communication between diverse systems.

The second hurdle includes privacy and security concerns. DID's core principles are to manage privacy and security, so the underlying blockchain technology and cryptographic methods must be robust enough against evolving cyber threats.

The third hurdle includes the regulatory and ethical considerations. Web 3.0 and DIDs raise questions about regulatory compliance, especially given the varied legal frameworks across different countries.

Summary

This chapter delved into the transformative shift toward an interconnected digital ecosystem, encompassing the metaverse, IoT, and Web 3.0. It discussed the digital frontier, emphasizing the pivotal role of DIDs in enhancing security, privacy, and user autonomy across emerging digital spaces. The chapter then explored the intricate interrelation between the metaverse, IoT, and Web 3.0 with DIDs, highlighting how these technologies will collectively forge a new paradigm of digital interaction and identity management.

Next the chapter covered the details of the convergence of the metaverse and DIDs, illustrating how DIDs can empower users with secure and portable identities within virtual environments. It also elaborated on the tangible benefits of DIDs within the metaverse, such as enhanced privacy, reduced fraud, and a more personalized user experience. In addition, the chapter discussed the practical applications of DIDs in the metaverse, providing examples of how they facilitate asset ownership, access control, and digital rights management.

Transitioning to IoT, the chapter underscored the critical need for DIDs in addressing the unique security and identity verification challenges posed by billions of interconnected devices. By implementing DIDs, IoT ecosystems can achieve a higher level of security and efficiency, enabling devices to authenticate and transact independently to pave the way for more autonomous and trusted digital environments.

The convergence of Web 3.0 and DIDs was another focal point of the chapter, which traced the evolution of Web 2.0's centralized platforms to Web 3.0's decentralized, user-centric framework. The chapter identified the core technologies driving Web 3.0, such as blockchain technology, and articulated how integrating DIDs into Web 3.0 could enhance user control over personal data, foster privacy, and facilitate a decentralized digital identity.

Overall, this chapter provided a comprehensive overview of the next-generation digital frontier, where DIDs will play a central role in bridging the diverse technological realms of the metaverse, IoT, and Web 3.0.

CHAPTER 10

Regulatory Landscape and Digital Rights

This chapter provides details of the regulatory landscape and digital rights with regard to decentralized identities (DIDs). It underscores the legal and ethical implications of DIDs, which are pivotal to governing digital identities. This chapter covers privacy laws, data protection, and regulatory compliance by global and regional governments.

Regulatory Landscape for DIDs

DIDs are still a nascent technology, and their regulatory framework is still evolving. However, various approaches are emerging globally, with different jurisdictions taking diverse stances. Globally, two general approaches are evolving.

Technology-Neutral Approach

Adopted by countries like UK and Singapore, the technology-neutral approach focuses on the implications of data protection and privacy on any digital identity system, rather than the specifics of the technology used. Technology-agnostic regulations can apply to a variety of systems handling personal data, including those using DIDs. This method allows for broader applicability and adaptability of laws, as they are not tied to the technical details of any specific technology, thereby enabling the regulations to remain relevant even as the technology evolves.

© Shivakumar R. Goniwada 2024
S. R. Goniwada, *Introduction to One Digital Identity*, https://doi.org/10.1007/979-8-8688-0255-3_10

Specific DID Regulations

The European Union (EU) and the United States represent jurisdictions where specific regulations for DIDs either are being considered or are in the process of development. These regulations cover various aspects of DIDs, such as the methods of DID issuance, the protocols for verification, the guidelines for secure storage, and the frameworks for determining liability in cases of data breaches or misuse. By focusing specifically on DIDs, these regulations aim to address the unique challenges and opportunities presented by this technology. This ensures that DIDs adhere to standards of identity verification and data security, while also considering the impact of these systems on user privacy and rights.

In both approaches, the central concern is to balance the innovative potential of DIDs with the need to protect an individual's privacy and data. The technology-neutral approach offers flexibility and broad applicability, while specific DID regulations provide a tailored framework that directly addresses the unique aspects of decentralized digital identities. As the use of DIDs continues to grow, it's likely that the industry will see further development and refinement in these regulatory approaches.

Global Regulatory Framework

The international regulatory landscape for DIDs is characterized by its diversity and lack of a unified framework. With the technology still in the early stages, various international organizations and individual countries are exploring different approaches to governance.

The efforts of international organizations like the World Wide Web Consortium (W3C), the Global Alliance for Digital Identity (GADI), and the International Organization for Standardization (ISO) highlight the growing importance and complexity of regulating DIDs. Each organization plays a unique role in shaping the global understanding and implementation of DIDs.

World Wide Web Consortium

The W3C established a Decentralized Identifier Working Group to develop technical standards, specifications, and best practices for DIDs. The focus of the W3C is to ensure interoperability and trust between different DID systems. By setting these standards, the

W3C aims to facilitate a uniform approach to DID technology, making it more accessible and reliable across different platforms and applications.[1]

Global Alliance for Digital Identity

GADI is engaging with governments and various stakeholders to develop a comprehensive framework for digital identities, which includes DIDs. The work involves creating guidelines and policies that ensure digital identities are secure and trustworthy. GADI's collaboration with governmental and nongovernmental entities is crucial for the widespread acceptance and integration of DIDs into the existing digital infrastructure.[2]

International Organization for Standardization

ISO is developing a standard for DIDs known as ISO/IEC 82848. This standard will address crucial aspects such as identification, verification, and privacy concerns related to DIDs. ISO's involvement is particularly important as it provides a global benchmark for the implementation of DIDs, aiming to harmonize the technology across various industries and countries.[3]

Regulatory Initiative by Region

The approach to regulating and implementing DIDs varies significantly across different regions, reflecting their unique legal, regulatory, and policy landscape.

European Union

In Europe, the approach to DIDs is being integrated into the broader framework of digital identity. The European Commission, as part of its commitment to a digital transformation, proposed a new framework for a European digital identity in June 2023.[4] This framework is designed to be available to all EU citizens, residents, and businesses, and it emphasizes the use of a personal digital wallet for various online and offline services across the EU.

---

[1] https://www.w3.org/TR/did-core/

[2] https://identity.foundation/

[3] https://www.iso.org/standard/82842.html

[4] https://www.european-digital-identity-regulation.com/

The EU Digital Identity Framework aims to provide a secure and trustworthy method for EU citizens and residents to identify themselves and confirm personal information. This initiative is a significant step toward enhancing the interoperability and trust of digital identities within the EU. The framework gives individuals full control over their data, deciding what information to share and with whom. This includes the ability to store and exchange information provided by governments and trusted private sources. The framework also includes practical applications such as opening bank accounts, filing tax returns, storing medical prescriptions, etc.

In terms of DIDs, this framework represents a move toward self-sovereign identity management, where individuals have greater control and autonomy over their digital identities. The European Commission also emphasizes the benefits of the EU digital identity in streamlining interactions with public and private services across member states, underlying its commitment to user privacy and data control.

Several EU states, including Estonia and Denmark, are piloting implementations of DID technology. These pilot projects are part of the larger effort to test and integrate digital identity wallets in real-life use cases across different sectors, involving private companies and public authorities from EU member states.

United States

In the United States, the regulatory landscape of DIDs is still developing, with no comprehensive federal regulations specifically addressing them. However, there are notable movements at the state level and in terms of broader cybersecurity frameworks.

States such as Wyoming and Arizona have taken proactive measures by passing laws that recognize blockchain-based records and electronics transactions.[5] These legislative efforts pave the way for the broader adoption of blockchain technologies, including DIDs, by establishing a legal framework that acknowledges and validates digital records and identities managed on blockchain platforms.

The National Institute of Standards and Technology (NIST) Cybersecurity Framework, a widely respected guide for managing cybersecurity risk, acknowledges the role of DIDs in identity management.[6] The inclusion of DIDs in the NIST framework signifies recognition at the federal level of the importance of innovative digital identity

---

[5] https://www.globallegalinsights.com/practice-areas/blockchain-laws-and-regulations/usa

[6] https://www.nist.gov/cyberframework

solutions in enhancing cybersecurity and identity management practices. By referencing DIDs, the NIST framework provides a level of validation and guidance for organizations considering the adoption of decentralized identity technologies.

India

India recently passed a bill named Digital Personal Data Protection (DPDP) Act.[7]

There is no direct reference to DIDs in this bill, but it proposes broader personal data protection. DIDs principles are aligned with the DPDP Act's focus on data minimization and user consent. It enables individuals to control their personal data by storing identity information in their own DIDs. This approach allows users to selectively share information with organizations.

The DPDP Act emphasizes the need for data localization, requiring that sensitive personal data be stored within India. DIDs can help comply with this requirement.

China

China is actively exploring the use of DIDs for various applications, including cross-border transactions and healthcare information sharing. The country's Blockchain-based Service Network (BSN) has developed RealDID,[8] a decentralized identity system.

RealDID allows users to register and log in to websites anonymously using DIDs and private keys to keep personal information separate from business data and transactions. This approach enhances data privacy and addresses concerns related to the misuse of personal data.

Africa

In Africa, DIDs are being explored as solutions to address various challenges. In Kenya, DIDs are being considered for land titling to streamline property ownership records and enhance transparency. Meanwhile, Rwanda is focusing on utilizing DIDs for financial inclusion, a move that could significantly improve access to financial services for its population.

---

[7] https://www.meity.gov.in/writereaddata/files/Digital%20Personal%20Data%20Protection%20Act%202023.pdf

[8] https://www.coindesk.com/policy/2023/12/12/chinas-ministry-of-public-security-launches-blockchain-based-real-name-decentralized-identifier-system/

Comparative Analysis of Regulatory Approaches

Table 10-1 is a comparative analysis of DID regulation across regions.

Table 10-1. *Regulatory Comparative Analysis*

Category	EU	US	Asia	Africa
Approach	Technology-neutral (focus on data protection and privacy)	State-by-state approach, evolving federal interest	Country-specific initiatives, varying levels of maturity	Early stage, pilot projects ongoing
Key Focus	Data security and privacy, interoperability, AML/CFT	Innovation, blockchain integration, pilot projects	Cross-border applications, digital inclusion, efficiency	Land titling, financial inclusion, identity management
Challenges	Harmonization across member states, balancing innovation with privacy	Lack of federal framework, navigating diverse state laws	Balancing economic opportunities with security concerns, developing technical standards	Building infrastructure, raising awareness, addressing access inequalities

Tools and Protocols for Interoperability in the DID Ecosystem

In the DID ecosystem, several tools and protocols will be instrumental in establishing a secure, efficient, and interoperable environment for managing digital identities. These components are designed to support the decentralized and user-centric nature of DIDs, ensuring that individuals have control over their own identity data while maintaining privacy and security. The following are the few tools and specifications that will enable DIDs to be successful in all areas.

DID Core Specifications

A foundational element of DID ecosystems is the DID specification itself, as defined by a standard organization like the W3C. This specification will outline how DIDs are created and resolved, updated, and deactivated, essentially providing the rulebook for DID governance.

DID Method and Registries

DID methods are specific implementations of the DID specification, tailored to different platforms or technologies. Each DID method will have its own registry, a decentralized database where DIDs and their corresponding DID documents are stored. Examples include methods based on blockchain technologies, where the registry might be a particular blockchain ledger.

DID Resolution Protocols

To use DIDs, systems need to be able to retrieve the corresponding DID document, which contains public keys and other control information. DID resolution protocols will be responsible for this, translating a DID into a DID document. This process involves querying the appropriate registry and ensuring that the DID document returned is authentic and up-to-date.

Verifiable Credentials

Verifiable credentials (VCs) are digital statements that are made by issuer about a subject, and they are essential part of the DID ecosystem. VCs can represent anything from driver's licenses to university degrees to health records. The use of VCs in conjunction with DIDs will allow for the secure and verifiable sharing of credentials without revealing unnecessary personal information.

Cryptographic Tools

Cryptography is pivotal in securing DIDs, acting as the core mechanism for ensuring safe communication, verifying identities, and maintaining the integrity of data within the DID ecosystem. At its essence, cryptography is a sophisticated and exclusive language, comprehensible only to authorize entities. It underpins the confidentiality of the system, ensuring that information is accessible only to those with the right cryptographic keys, thereby protecting sensitive information from unauthorized access or exposure.

Additionally, it plays a crucial role in authenticating identities. Cryptographic algorithms are used to create and verify digital signatures, linking DIDs to their rightful owners and preventing identity theft or impersonation. This process also ensures nonrepudiation, meaning that actions or transactions performed within the DID ecosystem can be unequivocally attributed to a specific entity, preventing denial of involvement or manipulation of data. Cryptography's role in DIDs is therefore multifaceted; it not only safeguards the privacy and security of the digital identities but also instills trust and reliability in the interactions and transactions that occur within these decentralized networks.

The following are the cryptographic methods that are used in DIDs:

- **Public-key cryptography:** This is a fundamental element in the management and security of DIDs. It operates on a dual-key mechanism, consisting of a public key and a private key, which together facilitate secure digital interactions. The public key can be thought of as a public visible lock; it's kept secret and solely in the procession of the key owner. This private key is used to decrypt the messages received and to authenticate the owner's identity, proving they are the legitimate controller of their DID. This system ensures secure communication, as only the intended recipient with the right private key can read the messages. Using public-key cryptography in DIDs thus offers a powerful tool for maintaining privacy, security, and trust in the digital realm.

- **Digital signature:** Digital signatures are an essential component in ensuring the authenticity and integrity of data in the DIDs. Functioning as the electronic equivalent of a handwritten signature, they provide a secure and verifiable way of confirming the identity of the signatory and the originality of the signed content. When a document or a piece of data is signed using a private key, it generates a unique digital fingerprint or signature, which is inextricably linked to the specific document and key used. This signature acts as a robust seal, affirming that the signatory is indeed the one who signed the document and that the document has remained unaltered since the time of signing. Anyone with access to the signatory's public key can verify the authenticity of the signature.

Interoperability Protocols

Since DIDs can exist across different methods and systems, interoperability protocols are crucial. These protocols ensure that a DID created in one ecosystem can be understood and utilized in another, facilitating cross-platform communication and validations.

Smart Contracts and Decentralized Applications

In blockchain-based DID ecosystems, smart contracts and dApps play a significant role. They enable automated, self-executing agreements and applications that interact with DIDs, further expanding the utility and functionality of the DID ecosystem.

Legal Challenges and Considerations

The integration of DIDs into identity management systems presents several legal challenges in areas such as privacy, intellectual property, liability, and enforcement. Let's look at each of these challenges.

Privacy and Data Protection

Privacy and data protection present complex challenges. First, data ownership is complicated by the fact that existing data protection regulations like GDPR or CCPA require a new interpretation or frameworks be applicable to DIDs. Additionally, DIDs could enable sophisticated tracking capabilities due to their inherent transparency, necessitating a careful balance between transparency benefits and individual privacy. Lastly, decentralized systems might introduce new vulnerabilities, making robust security measures and clear breach notification procedures essential to protect against and respond to data breaches.

Intellectual Property Rights

Ownership concerns extend to the underlying code and algorithms of DIDs, as well as the data stored within them, potentially leading to intellectual property (IP) infringements. The existence of multiple DID protocols and implementations further complicates matters, creating challenges related to standardization, interoperability, and a fragmented IP landscape. Additionally, for businesses, DIDs pose unique considerations for brand protection and trademark issues, necessitating a reevaluation of how DIDs might impact brands and the legalities surrounding them.

Liability and Enforcement

Liability and enforcement present significant challenges. Attribution and accountability are difficult due to the decentralized nature of DIDs, complicating efforts to identify and hold accountable parties responsible for malicious activities. Jurisdictional complexities arise since DIDs often transcend geographic boundaries, leading to enforcement actions and legal recourse that will span multiple legal systems. This global nature necessitates the development and implementation of specialized dispute resolution mechanisms to address disputes arising from the use of DIDs.

Digital Rights in the Context of DIDs

Decentralized identifiers usher in a new era of identity management, creating both exciting opportunities and complex challenges for digital rights. To understand this, we will look at digital rights in the context of the digital age.

Digital rights refers to the principles and policies that govern the use, security, privacy, and accessibility of digital identities and personal information online. With DIDs, these rights gain a new dimension as individuals gain more control over their digital identities. This shift necessitates a reevaluation of how we manage and protect these digital identities, ensuring that they are used ethically and responsibly, while also respecting individual privacy, freedom, and access in the digital world.

The following are the essential dimensions of digital rights:

- **Privacy and data protection:** Individuals have a right to control and access their personal data stored within DIDs. It includes the ability to opt out of unwanted data collection and to ensure the secure storage of this data. This approach aligns with broader digital rights, emphasizing the need for robust mechanisms to protect personal information from unauthorized access and breaches, while also providing users with the autonomy to manage their digital identities effectively.

- **Security and trust:** Users have the right to a system that is secure and reliable, safeguarding against breaches, fraud, and misuse. This includes robust cryptographic protections, vigilant monitoring for potential vulnerabilities, and swift response mechanisms to address any security incidents. Trust in DID systems also hinges on transparency about security protocols and practices, ensuring users feel confident in the safety and integrity of their digital identities.

- **Freedom of expression and association:** This right entails the ability to express oneself and associate freely online without the fear of surveillance or censorship that might arise from DID usage. It emphasizes the need for DIDs to be designed in a way that supports and protects a user's freedom online, ensuring they can communicate and connect without undue monitoring or restrictions.

- **Transparency and accountability:** Users have the right to understand how their DIDs are used, who is using them, and for what purposes. This transparency is essential for building trust in the DID ecosystem. Additionally, there must be a clear mechanism in place to hold any party responsible for the misuse of DIDs.

- **Interoperability and portability:** Interoperability is vital for preventing users from being locked into a specific platform or ecosystem. It enables a more user-centric approach to digital identity management, where individuals have the freedom and capability to choose and transition between different services without losing control of their digital identities.

- **Right to self-determination and agency:** This encompasses the ability to make informed decisions about the use of one's digital identity, including the option to opt out of specific identifiers. This right ensures that users can manage their digital presence according to their preference and needs.

The Intersection of DIDs and Digital Rights

The adoption of DIDs marks a pivotal shift toward more secure, private, and user-controlled digital environments. DIDs are not just technical tool; they are instruments of empowerment, enabling individuals to reclaim their digital rights in a landscape that has long been dominated by centralized entities.

The following list explains how DIDs enhance digital rights:

- **Privacy:** One of the most critical benefits of DIDs is the enhancement of online privacy. Existing online identifiers, like email addresses or social media profiles, are often linked to extensive personal data. DIDs, however, decouple personal data from these identifiers. By doing so, DIDs help mask online activities, making it harder for these activities to be traced back to an individual. This greatly reduces the risks associated with surveillance and profiling by external entities.

- **Control:** DIDs empower users by giving them complete control over their digital identities. Unlike a centralized system, where users must abide by the terms and conditions of service providers, DIDs enable individuals to decide what information they want to share, with whom, and for what purpose.

- **Security:** The security of DIDs is based on cryptography. By configuring advanced cryptographic techniques, DIDs offer a robust defense against identity fraud and theft.

- **Inclusivity:** DIDs are inherently inclusive. Since DIDs can be created and managed by anyone with an Internet connection and little knowledge, they transcend geographical, social, and economic barriers.

- **Transparency:** Another key aspect of DIDs is their ability to increase transparency in the digital domain. Users can track how their data is used, shared, or accessed, which is often not possible in centralized systems. This level of transparency ensures a higher degree of accountability, particularly in how personal data is handled by different online services and platforms.

- **Revoking subscription:** In the DID framework, users have the ability to revoke or modify their association with certain services. For instance, if a user decides to discontinue a service or no longer trusts a particular platform, they can revoke the platform access with their DIDs. This process is typically facilitated by updating the DID document, a record associated with the DID that specifies the public key and access rights.

Ownership and Control of Digital Content

The increasingly decentralized digital landscape requires new approaches to IP management. DIDs, with their focus on individual control and self-sovereign identity, offer a solution for managing ownership and control of digital content. Each piece of digital content is linked to a unique DID, essentially a digital identifier that is controlled solely by the content creator or owner. This ensures that the ownership and rights associated with the digital content are explicitly and securely established. Owners can then manage their content directly, exercising control over its distribution, usage, and monetization.

For example, Nikki creates a piece of digital artwork, and then she can assign a DID to this art. This DID not only signifies ownership but also contains metadata about the artwork, such as creation date, ownership history, and usage rights. This metadata can be dynamically updated, reflecting any changes in ownership or rights over time.

As another example, using DIDs to manage digital content enables more nuanced and flexible licensing options. Nikki can set specific permissions for each piece of content, defining who can access, share, or modify her work. These permissions are directly linked to the DID, ensuring they are respected and enforced across platforms.

Collaboration and attribution in creative projects are also enhanced through DIDs. Let's consider Nikki and her friends together write a white paper; in this case, each contributor can have their part tagged with their unique DID, ensuring proper attribution and potential compensation based on the agreed-upon terms. This clarity in attribution helps in maintaining transparency and fairness in collaborative environments.

In the case of disputes, such as copyright infringement or unauthorized usage, DIDs provide a reliable and verifiable record of ownership and permissions, simplifying the resolution process. Since the information linked to a DID is tamper-proof and transparent, it serves as a credible source of evidence in legal scenarios.

DIDs can be used to develop a decentralized marketplace for digital content and eliminate the need for intermediaries. This allows creators such as musicians to sell or license their work directly to consumers or users. This direct approach not only reduces costs associated with middlemen but also ensures that creators retain a larger portion of the revenue generated from their work.

Case Studies

There are a few platforms that already integrate DIDs to help manage digital rights.

- **Mycelia:** This platform is used in the music industry and leverages DIDs to revolutionize how music ownership and rights are managed. By using DIDs, Mycelia allows artists to register and track the ownership of their music creations. The system empowers musicians with direct control over how their work is used, shared, and monetized. Through Mycelia, DIDs act as digital passports for each piece of music, containing detailed rights information, usage policies, and ownership history.[9]

- **Verisart:** Verisart is a blockchain-based platform that utilizes DIDs to tackle challenges in the digital art world, particularly issues of authenticity and ownership. By assigning DIDs to digital artworks, Verisart creates a secure and immutable record of provenance and ownership. This technology significantly reduces the risk of forgery and fraud in the art market. For collectors and artists alike, Verisart provides a trusted mechanism to verify the authenticity of digital art. The DID linked to each artwork contains verifiable details about the creator, history, and authenticity of the art.[10]

Summary

This chapter offered a comprehensive overview of the complex regulatory environment surrounding DIDs and digital rights. This chapter began by introducing the regulatory landscape for DIDs and highlighting how different jurisdictions are developing frameworks to govern this emerging technology. It also provided insight into the global regulatory framework, underscoring the challenges and opportunities in creating standards that can be universally applied, given the decentralized nature of DIDs.

---

[9] http://myceliaformusic.org/
[10] https://verisart.com/

Further, this chapter delved into regulatory initiatives by region, offering a comparative analysis of approaches taken by various governments and regulatory bodies. It also covered the tools and protocols that will be essential to achieving interoperability in DID systems.

The chapter also covered the implications of DIDs in terms of privacy, security, and compliance with existing laws. The chapter provided details of the complexities of aligning DIDs with data protection regulations such as GDPR, DPDP, etc., and the implications of blockchain technology in a legal context.

This chapter also provided insight into digital rights in the context of DIDs, examining how DIDs intersect with the concept of digital rights. It discussed the implication of DIDs on ownership and control of digital content.

Overall, this chapter provided a nuanced understanding of the regulatory and legal landscape of DIDs.

CHAPTER 11

The Human Aspects - Societal and Psychological Implication

This chapter explains the societal and psychological implications of the modern digital world and how decentralized identities (DIDs) are reshaping human interactions and self-perception.

This chapter answers the following questions:

- What is identity fatigue, and how does it manifest in your online behavior?

- What are the societal and psychological factors that contribute to identity fatigue?

- How do centralized platforms and data exploitation fuel this phenomenon?

- How does the constant pressure to compare, compete, and curate online personas lead to anxiety and disconnection?

- How do DIDs empower a user to break free from the silos and manipulation of centralized platforms?

Introduction to Digital Authenticity

In the modern digital era, the Internet, initially celebrated as a liberating force for self-expression and connection, has paradoxically evolved into a complex and sometimes treacherous landscape where the notion of authenticity is increasingly

213

© Shivakumar R. Goniwada 2024
S. R. Goniwada, *Introduction to One Digital Identity*, https://doi.org/10.1007/979-8-8688-0255-3_11

contested. This shift is largely attributed to the rise of social media and online platforms, where the ability to curate and manipulate personal identities has become both a norm and a necessity.

The personas that people craft online are often meticulously constructed, showcasing highlight reels of life rather than the unfiltered realities. This phenomenon stems from the desire to present an idealized version of oneself to the world, influenced by various factors such as social comparison, the pursuit of social validation, and the inherent nature of social media platforms that encourage sharing positive and noteworthy moments. These online personas can significantly differ from the complex and nuanced realities of everyday life. There are many factors that influence online personas, including social comparison, social validation, and platform dynamics.

Two examples of personas are described here:

- **Travel enthusiast**

  Online persona: Posts are primarily breathtaking travel photos, adventurous experiences, and luxurious accommodations, presenting a life of constant exploration and leisure

  Unfiltered reality: Might not showcase the challenges of travel, such as the planning process, costs, jet lag, or moments of loneliness, reflecting only the glamorous side of travel.

- **Fitness guru**

  Online persona: Shares pictures and videos of workouts, healthy meals, and physique, suggesting a disciplined and healthy-focused lifestyle

  Unfiltered reality: Rarely discusses the day's lacking motivation, the struggle with diet restrictions, or the journey of overcoming fitness plateaus, focusing mainly on achievements and progress

This divergence from one's true self can lead to what is described as an existential crisis of authenticity.

The crisis stems from the conflict between the authentic self, the person one truly is, with all their flaws, complexities, and mundane realities; and the digital self, which is often an idealized, edited, and selectively presented version. The pressure to maintain these curated personas can be immense, leading to psychological stress and identity confusion. People may find themselves constantly comparing their real lives to the seemingly perfect lives portrayed by other online, exacerbating feelings of inadequacy, jealous, and dissatisfaction. Furthermore, the digital realm offers a level of anonymity and detachment that can sometimes encourage inauthentic interactions, where individuals may say or do things they wouldn't in physical settings.

This crisis is not just a personal issue; it has broader societal implications. The divergence between online personas and true selves can erode trust in online interactions and contribute to a wider culture of superficiality and disconnection, despite the Internet's original promise of fostering deeper connections.

Promoting Genuine Expressions

As I mentioned in earlier chapters, DIDs have the potential to reclaim control and promote genuine expression online. Existing digital identities are controlled by centralized platforms, which collect and monetize our data. DID flips this approach, putting individuals in control. Imagine instead owning your own identity data stored securely on a blockchain, accessible only through your unique cryptographic key. This empowers you to decide who sees what information, when, and for what purpose. No more data scraping, targeted advertising, or hidden algorithms dictating your online experience.

This control translates to genuine expression. Sharing becomes your choice, free from platform manipulation or fear of data misuse. You can build a digital persona that truly reflects your values and beliefs, unconstrained by expectations or societal pressures. Imagine expressing unpopular opinions without fear of repercussions, engaging in sensitive discussions without surveillance, or exploring niche communities without algorithmic censorship. DIDs give you the freedom to be your authentic self in the digital realm.

The Impact of Social Media on Self-Perception

Social media has fundamentally reshaped how we understand ourselves and others. Existing social dynamics have been transformed, with curated online personas replacing face-to-face interactions and algorithms dictating which voices are heard and whose are silenced. This digital landscape can often distort self-perception, leading to anxieties around online validation and pressure to conform to unrealistic expectations.

The growing disconnect between people's real-life identities and their digital selves can lead to issues like social comparison, where constant exposure to idealized versions of others on social media platforms can negatively impact mental health and self-esteem. The pressure to maintain a certain image online can also lead to lack of authenticity, as individuals may feel compelled to present only their best selves, omitting realities that don't align with the desired perception.

DIDs disrupt this paradigm and instigate cultural shifts. By handing control of our data and online presence back to individuals, DIDs empower us to create authentic digital identities that are not beholden to centralized platforms and their manipulative algorithms. This shift could redefine social dynamics, fostering communities built on shared values and genuine connection rather than superficial "likes" and manufactured trends.

Identity Fatigue: When Being Online Hurts Our Well-Being

Centralized platforms, characterized by their dominant algorithms and voracious appetite for user data, significantly contribute to the phenomenon of identity fatigue. These platforms function selectively by amplifying content that resonates with a user's pre-existing beliefs and preferences, while simultaneously suppressing a variety of perspectives. This process reinforces existing biases and hinders genuine identity exploration by constantly validating a user's current viewpoints.

A critical aspect of this environment in social comparison. Platforms curate feeds that often display idealized portrayals of other's lives, leading users to perceive their own experiences as less fulfilling or successful. This curated reality can trigger feelings of inadequacy, anxiety, and dissatisfaction, as users compare themselves to these seemingly flawless online personas.

The role of algorithms in shaping online experiences, especially on social media platforms, is profound. These algorithms are engineered to capture and retain user attention by personalizing content feeds based on individual preferences, behaviors, and interactions. This personalization can inadvertently amplify negative emotions by creating echo chambers of similar content, which can reinforce feelings of envy, self-doubt, comparison, and disconnection from reality.

Here are a few types of algorithms related to this dynamics:

- **Content recommendation algorithms:** The purpose of this type of algorithm is to suggest content that users are likely to engage with, based on their past behavior, engagement history, and preferences. For example, a social media platform might use these algorithms to show posts, videos, or images that are similar to what a user has liked or spent time viewing, potentially emphasizing highlight reels from other's lives that can induce comparison and envy.

- **Engagement optimization algorithms:** The purpose of this type of algorithm is to maximize user engagement (likes, comments, and shares) by prioritizing content that is performing well among similar users. For example, posts that receive a lot of engagement quickly after being published are more likely to be shown to more users, which can skew the perception of popularity or success, contributing to feelings of inadequacy in users whose content doesn't perform well.

- **Behavioral tracking and profiling algorithms:** The purpose of this type of algorithm is to collect and analyze data on a user's behavior, preferences, and interactions to build detailed profiles for targeted content delivery. These algorithms help to predict what type of content a user will find engaging or provoking, potentially leading to a cycle where the user is repeatedly exposed to content that triggers negative emotions.

- **Echo chamber algorithms:** The purpose of this type of algorithm is to create a feed that reflects the user's existing beliefs, interests, and biases by filtering out dissenting information. This algorithm reinforces a user's viewpoints or interests without introducing diverse perspectives; these algorithms can isolate users in a bubble of content that reinforces feelings of disconnections from broader, perhaps more balanced, realities.

- **Sentiment analysis and emotional targeting algorithms:** The purpose of this type of algorithm is to understand the emotional tone of content and how users react to different types of content and then use the understanding to target users with content that elicits specific emotional responses. This platform might use sentiment analysis to identify content that evokes strong emotional reactions like joy, surprise, sadness, etc., and algorithmically prioritize content likely to keep users engaged, even if it means perpetuating negative emotional cycles.

Furthermore, the centralized control of these platforms means they have substantial influence over how users' identities are presented and perceived online. They effectively dictate the terms of digital social interactions, filtering and shaping the content that users see and engage with. This manipulation reduces user control over their own digital narratives, contributing to feelings of alienation and inauthenticity. Users often find themselves projecting a carefully curated persona that may not align with their true self, leading to a blurring of the lines between their authentic identity and their online image.

In the realm of digital identities, these algorithms manipulate user experiences and emotions. The goal is to maximize user engagement profit, often at the cost of well-being. This results in users feeling exhausted and disconnected from their authentic selves, trapped in a cycle of identity fatigue driven by the very platforms they frequent.

Sustainable Engagement in the Centralized Identity

Because of the overwhelming effects of identity fatigue in the centralized identity, there's a rising trend toward digital wellness. Users are actively seeking a more balanced and fulfilling online experience.

The following are a few techniques that users can practice:

- **Mindful engagement:** This encourages users to interact with content that is meaningful and enriching, rather than that which induces stress or negative comparisons.

- **Conscious content consumption and healthy boundaries:** Individuals can adopt several strategies such as doing a digital detox, customizing notification settings, and selectively unfollowing or muting accounts. These strategies help individuals regain control over their digital lives and reduce the constant bombardment of stimuli that can lead to fatigue.

- **Shift to authentic online communities:** There is growing movement toward building decentralized platforms, where an individual can find and build diverse, authentic, and like-minded online communities. These spaces are often centered around shared interest and values, rather than algorithmically curated content. Such decentralized platforms encourage genuine connections, respectful discourse, and vulnerability, countering the performative nature of mainstream social media.

Decentralized Identities to the Rescue: Empowering Authentic Connections

A DID is an improved and better solution to combat the challenges of identity fatigue and the restrictive nature of centralized digital platforms. DIDs represent a significant shift toward a more autonomous and privacy-centric online experience.

As mentioned in earlier chapters, a DID is part of the concept of self-sovereign identifiers (SSIs), which are unique, cryptographically secure keys owned and controlled by the individual, not a centralized authority or platform like your email for your social media account. This eliminates the dependence on centralized platforms, shattering the data silos that trap users and fragment their online lives. With DIDs, users move beyond walled gardens and embrace a distributed, user-centric identity landscape.

Another principle of DIDs is that they empower users to decouple identity from the data. Rather than surrendering vast amounts of personal data to various platforms, users can choose precisely what data to share and with whom. For example, you could verify your age on a website without revealing your full date of birth or share specific educational qualifications with an employer without exposing your entire academic history. DIDs make such granular control a reality.

Other principles of DIDs are trust and transparency. DIDs can be linked to verifiable claims issued by trusted entities, such as universities or employers. This allows users to present their credentials and qualifications without relying on centralized platforms. For example, a user can present verifiable, tamper-proof badges to showcase professional skills or secure transcripts for academic achievements.

While DIDs are empowering digital identity management, their widespread adoption and integration into mainstream platforms pose challenges. Technical, regulatory, and user adoption hurdles need to be addressed for DIDs to realize their full potential. Nevertheless, DIDs offer a compelling vision for a future where online identities are more authentic, self-controlled, and respectful of individual privacy. These changes will promise to alleviate identity fatigue and enable more meaningful and secure connections in the digital world.

Navigating the New Landscape: Cultivating Digital Wellness with DIDs

The integration of DIDs into the digital realm offers a new avenue for cultivating digital wellness, but it requires mindful engagement to fully harness its benefits. DIDs present unique opportunities to reshape online interactions.

DIDs don't eliminate the need for conscious online engagement. Users must still practice mindfulness around screen time, curate information sources critically, and set boundaries. However, DIDs empower users to personalize these practices. For example, they can filter notifications based on verifiable data from issues you trust or restrict access to specific applications during designated focus periods. DIDs put the power back into the users' hand, allowing users to tailor the online environment to support individual needs and promote digital wellness.

DIDs facilitate the creation of trust-based online communities. By enabling the verification of claims and credentials, they pave the way for more meaningful and authentic connections. Users can engage with others whose skills and qualifications are verifiable and authentic, fostering trust and collaboration in online spaces. This shift from anonymity and superficial interactions to verified and meaningful connections can profoundly impact the quality of online communities.

With DIDs, individuals can move beyond the constraints of curated online personas dictated by platform algorithms. They allow for sharing the verifiable aspects of one's life and experiences, leading to more authentic self-expression. For example, artists could use cryptographic proofs to validate the originality of their work, or writers could utilize tamper-proof timestamps to assert authorship. This autonomy in self-presentation enriches online identity and fosters a more diverse and genuine digital landscape.

DIDs don't just facilitate online engagement; they also have the potential to bridge the gap between digital and physical interactions. They can be used to enhance real-world experiences, such as using verified online credentials for community volunteering or leveraging digital networks for organizing physical events. This integration of the digital and physical aspects of life encourages a more holistic approach to identity and community engagement.

The journey with DIDs is just beginning, and its path will be paved by collective choices and mindful actions. By embracing DIDs with intention and awareness, users can cultivate a digital landscape that respects users' autonomy.

Reclaiming Users' Online Selves

DIDs are not merely a technological solution; they represent a philosophical shift toward reclaiming users' online selves. This journey must start with a reassessment of values and priorities. Users must step back from the algorithm-driven echo chambers and ask, "What kind of digital citizen do I want to be?" DIDs empower users to answer this question by giving them control over the data, interactions, and narratives that the user builds. They become tools for a mindful online presence, allowing users to curate experiences that nourish a user's well-being and align with their authentic self.

The transformative potential of DIDs extends beyond their technical capabilities, reaching into the realm of human connection. The use of verifiable claims through DIDs can encourage empathy and vulnerability, fostering spaces for genuine interaction beyond the surface level of curated personas. For example, verifying volunteer experiences can help users connect with like-minded individuals for community projects, and displaying verifiable badges can showcase one's passion for a cause, inspiring others and fostering deeper connections.

However, the quest for authenticity in the digital realm is an ongoing journey. DIDs come with the responsibility of using them ethically and thoughtfully. Users must guard against the temptation to weaponize verification or fall into the trap of self-quantification. Instead, users can use DIDs to tell their stories with nuance and vulnerability, sharing their passions, experiences, and imperfections. In doing so, users contribute to a more human online world, where connections thrive on shared experiences and empathy, not curated feeds and algorithmic manipulation.

DIDs are not a magic wand to solve all users' online woes. DIDs are a powerful tool but one that requires conscious effort and ethical considerations. By approaching DIDs with intentionally, mindfulness, and humanness, you can reclaim your online self and build a digital future that celebrates authenticity, connection, and well-being.

Summary

This chapter delved into the complexities of digital authenticity and the quest for genuine self-expression within the online realm. It addressed how social media platforms, through their design and algorithms, significantly impact self-perception. In fact, they often lead to identity fatigue, a state where individuals feel overwhelmed by the need to manage and present multiple facets of their identity in a manner that is both coherent and appealing to their online audience. This discourse extended into a critique of centralized identity systems, which, while facilitating engagement, often do so at the cost of authentic personal expression.

This chapter then explored DIDs as a promising avenue for fostering more genuine connections and empowering users to reclaim control over their online selves. DIDs, by design, encourage a digital environment where users can engage sustainably, prioritizing digital wellness and enabling individuals to present a more authentic version of themselves without the pressures imposed by centralized platforms.

Through this lens, the chapter underscored the critical need for a shift toward platforms and practices that support the holistic well-being of individuals in the digital age, advocating for a reclamation of personal agency in online identities and interactions.

CHAPTER 12

Peering into the Future - Next Frontiers in Digital Identity

This chapter explores the future of digital identities. It specifically outlines the promise held by technologies such as AI, quantum computing, and edge computing.

We will also answer the following questions:

- How are emerging technologies reshaping the concept of digital identities?

- How are emerging technologies reshaping the way you interact online?

- How will interstellar identities in space colonization work?

- How can AI be adopted in a decentralized ecosystem?

- How can biometric fusion be used?

- Will the future be a utopian or dystopian world?

This chapter provides a comprehensive understanding of what the future of digital identities might hold and the challenges and opportunities.

© Shivakumar R. Goniwada 2024
S. R. Goniwada, *Introduction to One Digital Identity*, https://doi.org/10.1007/979-8-8688-0255-3_12

Future Trends and Innovations

Digital identities are poised to undergo significant transformations, driven by the integration of advanced technologies such as predictive models, behavioral biometrics, and the synergistic use of 5G, edge computing, and quantum computing. Here are few details:

- **5G:** 5G represents a major evolution in mobile technology, building on the foundation laid by 4G LTE to dramatically enhance network performance and efficiency. This fifth-generation technology is engineered to support a 100+ fold increase in traffic capacity, allowing networks to handle an ever-expanding volume of data transmission seamlessly. 5G provides significantly reduced latency, which refers to the delay before a transfer of data begins following an instruction. This improvement is critical for real-time applications such as augmented reality (AR), virtual reality (VR), and autonomous vehicles, where immediate response is essential.

- **Edge computing:** This is a transformative approach to network architecture, focusing on decentralizing the processing of data by bringing computational capabilities closer to the data sources, such as IoT devices, sensors, and local edge servers. By processing data near its origin, edge computing enables faster insights into the data collected, significantly improving the response time for real-time applications.

- **Quantum computing:** When faced with complex problems that overwhelm classical supercomputers, the limitations of these powerful machines become apparent. Supercomputers, despite their vast array of CPUs and GPUs, operate on binary code and rely on transistor technology. The challenges include accurately modeling the behavior of atoms within molecules due to the complex interplay of electrons and detecting nuanced patterns of fraud in financial transactions. These issues push the boundaries of what classical computer can handle, primarily because traditional binary systems have limitations in processing and simulating the probabilistic nature of quantum interactions. Quantum computers, which utilize quantum bits (*qubits*) to perform calculations, represent a paradigm shift in tackling these problems. By leveraging the principles of quantum mechanics, quantum computing offers the potential to process information in ways that classical systems cannot, enabling solutions to problems previously considered unsolvable.

Predictive Models

Predictive models powered by artificial intelligence and machine learning are set to revolutionize how we approach identity verification and fraud detection. By analyzing patterns and behaviors over time, these models can anticipate potential security breaches or fraudulent activities, offering a proactive stance in identity management. This shift from reactive to predictive security measures could significantly reduce the incidence of identity theft and unauthorized access.

Complementing predictive models is the emerging field of behavioral biometrics. Unlike traditional biometrics like fingerprints, eye scans, etc., which rely on static physical characteristics, behavioral biometrics focus on unique patterns in human activities: the way someone types, swipes on screen, or even walks. This form of biometric authentication provides a continuous verification layer, ensuring that the person accessing the service is indeed the authorized user. Biometric authentication is dynamic, is harder to replicate, and adapts over time, offering a more nuanced and secure approach to identity verification.

The role of 5G, edge computing, and quantum computing are equally pivotal in this evolution. 5G networks, with their high speed and lower latency, enable real-time data processing and rapid communication between devices. This is crucial for decentralized systems, where immediate and reliable data transfer is essential for maintaining the integrity and responsiveness of an identity management system.

Edge computing, on other hand, pushes data processing close to where it's needed: at the edge of the network, near the user. This decentralization of computing resources aligns perfectly with decentralized identity systems. It allows for faster processing of biometric data, reduces latency, and enhances privacy, as sensitive data doesn't need to travel back and forth to a central server.

Quantum computing presents both opportunities and challenges for decentralized identifiers (DIDs). On one hand, its unparallel processing power could break current cryptographic methods, posing a threat to the security of identity systems. On the other hand, it offers the potential for developing new, quantum-resistant cryptographic algorithms. This could lead to significantly more secure identity verification processes, ensuring the long-term resilience of DID systems against emerging computational threats.

The future of DIDs is being shaped by these emerging technologies. Predictive models and behavioral biometrics enhance security and the user experience, while 5G and edge computing contribute to system efficiency and responsiveness. Quantum computing is set to redefine the cryptographic landscape, ensuring the robustness of identity systems against future threats.

Quantum-Resistant Cryptographic Algorithms

The rise of quantum computing presents significant challenges to current public-key cryptographic systems, which rely on the computational difficulty of problems such as integer factorization, which are vulnerable to quantum attacks. To counter this, quantum-resistant cryptographic algorithms have been analyzed based on mathematical problems believed to be secure against quantum computing threats. These include lattice-based and code-based cryptography, among others. The National Institute of Standards and Technology (NIST) has recently selected four algorithms for standardization in response to these challenges.

- CRYSTALS-Kyber for encryption purposes

- CRYSTALS-Dilithium, FALCON, and SPHINCS+ for digital signatures

The transition to quantum-resistant cryptography is essential but will require adjustments in current cryptographic practices to ensure the protection of sensitive information in the quantum era.

Beyond the Blockchain

The future of DIDs extends far beyond the realm of blockchain technology, as cutting-edge technologies are emerging to redefine security, privacy, and user control.

Quantum computing represents a paradigm shift in computational power and efficiency. It's built to process complex algorithms, and unprecedented speed poses both a challenge and an opportunity for identity security. As I mentioned, quantum computing could potentially break many of the cryptographic protocols that current security systems rely on, making existing encryption methods obsolete. This threat necessitates the development of quantum-resistant cryptographic techniques, which are already in progress. Quantum computing also offers new avenues for securing digital identities. For example, quantum key distribution (QKD) provides a method for sharing encryption keys that are theoretically immune to interception, ensuring a level of security that is currently unattainable with classical computing methods.

Another emerging technology is synthetic DNA storage with significant implications for biometric data storage and security. DNA, with its high-density storage capacity, can hold an immense amount of information in a remarkably small physical space, and its longevity far exceeds that of traditional data storage mediums. In the context of biometric evolution, this means that individual's biometric data could be encoded into synthetic DNA, offering a highly secure and long-lasting method of storing sensitive identity information. This approach is inherently more secure than current digital storage solutions in blockchain, as DNA data storage is not susceptible to traditional hacking methods. Additionally, as biometric technology evolves to recognize more complex patterns, including genetic markers, synthetic DNA could provide a way to store and manage these sophisticated biometric profiles, further enhancing the security and accuracy of identity verification processes.

Looking Way Ahead into the Unknown

As we gaze into the future landscape of digital identities, it becomes clear that this field is on the cusp of profound transformation, shaped by rapid technological advancements and changing societal needs.

Interoperable Ecosystems

The future of digital identity is steering toward the creation of interoperable ecosystems, with seamless and borderless exchanges of identity information. This change is powered by robust open standards and collaborative governance models, fundamentally altering how nations, corporations, and individuals interact in the digital realm.

In these interoperable ecosystems, the traditional silos that once segregated identity data across different platforms and geographical boundaries are crumbling. Instead, a web of trusted identity network will emerge, facilitated by universal standards and protocols that ensure compatibility and security across diverse systems. These standards are not just technical specifications; they are the result of global collaboration and consensus among various stakeholders, including governments, technology companies, and civil society organizations. This collaborative approach is crucial for addressing complex issues such as privacy, security, and user consent in a unified manner.

Interoperable ecosystems enable a more efficient and user-friendly experience. For example, a user could use their digital identity to seamlessly access services across different countries and sectors without needing to repeatedly undergo identity verifications. This fluidity is particularly impactful in areas like international travel, e-commerce, healthcare, and cross-border financial transactions, where a streamlined identity verification process could significantly enhance efficiency and security.

AI-Powered Trust Framework

The use of AI-powered trust frameworks signifies a shift in how security protocols are managed and how user experiences are personalized in the digital ecosystem. At the core of this is advanced machine learning algorithms, which are trained on vast amounts of anonymized data to dynamically adjust security measures and tailor user experiences to each user.

These AI frameworks are adept at identifying and evolving patterns of behavior and risk. Unlike traditional security models that rely on static credentials, such as passwords or security questions, these frameworks assess risk and trustworthiness in real time. This approach considers a multitude of factors, from user behavior patterns to the context of each interaction. For example, when unusual or potential risky behavior is detected, the system can instantly modify security protocols by requiring additional authentication steps. This dynamic adjustment not only bolsters security but also significantly enhances the user experience.

Biometric Fusion

Biometric fusion changes how identity verification is occurring by combining multiple biometric modalities, such as fingerprint scans, iris recognition, gait analysis, and voice verification. This creates a comprehensive, multilayered authentication system. In this advanced system, each biometric element plays a critical role. Fingerprint scans and iris recognition are well-established methods known for their high accuracy and reliability. However, when fused with gait analysis and voice verification, the system gains an additional layer of security. Gait analysis, the study of individual's walking pattern, adds a subtle yet powerful identifier that is difficult to mimic or replicate.

Artificial Intelligence: The Custodian of Digital Self

In the evolving landscape of digital identity, AI is emerging as a pivotal custodian of digital identity. AI systems are being designed to act as vigilant protectors of digital identities, employing advanced algorithms to monitor, detect, and respond to any threats or anomalies. This includes protecting against identity theft, unauthorized access, and various forms of cyber fraud. By continuously learning and adapting to new security threats, AI offers a dynamic defense mechanism that is far more advanced than static or rule-based systems.

Beyond mere protection, AI is becoming an advisor in identity management. It personalizes user experiences by understanding individual preferences and behaviors, thus enhancing convenience and efficiency. For example, AI can streamline authentication processes for trusted users or adjust security protocols based on contextual risk assessments.

However, the integration of AI into digital identity management brings forth significant ethical considerations, particularly regarding identity bias. AI systems, like any technology, can inherit biases present in their training data or algorithms. This could lead to unfair or discriminatory practices, where certain individuals or groups might be wrongly identified, excluded, or unfairly treated by automated systems. Addressing these concerns necessitates the development of ethical AI frameworks that prioritize fairness, transparency, and accountability. Rigorous testing and continuous refinement of AI systems are needed to ensure they do not perpetuate existing biases. Moreover, there is a need for diverse and inclusive datasets and algorithmic auditing to identify and mitigate potential biases. This ethical approach to AI in digital identity management is crucial to ensure that these technologies are equitable and do not inadvertently harm or disadvantage any user.

Interstellar Identity: Speculating on Space Colonization

As humanity stands on the brink of space colonization, the concept of interstellar identities emerges as a critical aspect of establishing and managing off-world communities. The creation of identity systems for these communities presents unique challenges and opportunities beyond what we encounter on Earth. Such systems must be robust and flexible enough to accommodate the conditions and societal structures that will evolve in extraterrestrial environments.

In these off-world communities, identity systems will play a pivotal role in ensuring the smooth functioning of societal and governance structures. They need to be designed not just to handle basic identification and verification but also to integrate with the diverse systems that will govern life in space, such as access to resources, healthcare, and habitat management. These systems might incorporate advanced biometrics and AI to adapt to the unique environmental and physiological changes humans may experience in space, such as altered physical features due to different gravity conditions.

Interplanetary Interoperability

Imagine a future where individuals can seamlessly navigate between these extraterrestrial locales, with their identities readily recognized and verified across different planetary jurisdictions. This vision hinges on the development of an advanced, universally accepted identity framework capable of operating across the vast expanse of space.

Central to this system would be an interoperable blockchain-based system or quantum-resistant cryptography, providing a backbone for a secure and universal identity framework. Blockchain technology, with its decentralized and tamper-proof ledger, is ideally suited for creating a unified identity system that is both secure and transparent. Quantum-resistant cryptography comes into play as a necessary safeguard against the potential vulnerabilities posed by quantum computing. Given the rapid advancements in quantum technology, any interplanetary identity system must be future-proofed against the immense processing power of quantum computers.

The interoperable identity systems would not only facilitate the practical aspects of interstellar traveler, such as access control and resource allocation, but also underpin legal and social structures of off-world communities. It would support the administration of interstellar rights and responsibilities, providing a consistent basis of governance and legal processes across jurisdiction.

Biometric Redefinition

The shift to extraterrestrial habitats brings about a redefinition of biometric identification, driven by the need to adapt to the unique and harsh realities of space environments. In the realm of lunar outposts, Martian settlements, or other celestial bodies, traditional biometrics such as fingerprints might prove unreliable because of factors such as spacesuits or altered skin conditions due to various conditions and atmosphere. This necessitates the exploration and adoption of biometric identifiers that are tailored to the challenges and peculiarities of space environments.

There are various options available like retina scans to create a biometric system with psychological responses to specific stellar radiation, for example.

The topic of living in space may be far-fetched, but considering the current pace of innovation, it could be possible in the near future.

Utopia or Dystopia: Scenarios of Future Societies

In the future, using decentralized identities could create a utopian environment or lead to dystopian control. Each societal construct presents a vastly different scenario shaped by technology and human choices. Fictional narratives and thought experiments serve as powerful tools to explore these potential futures, especially in the context of how DIDs might play a role in future governance.

In the utopian vision, DIDs act as a catalyst for empowered citizenship and collaborative governance. Individuals possess complete control over their data through SSI wallets, which hold not just financial assets but also crucial societal tokens like voting rights and educational credentials. This empowers citizens to actively participate in the governance process, casting informed votes on local proposals and directly influencing policy decisions. This also enables streamlined access to public services and reduced bureaucratic inefficiencies. This could create a more engaged and empowered people, where governance is participatory and inclusive.

In the dystopian version of the future, the same technology and processes could be twisted for oppressive means. A dystopian society might misuse decentralized identity systems for pervasive surveillance and control. In this scenario, while the technology is inherently secure and decentralized, it could be implemented in a way that infringes on privacy and individual freedoms. You can look at the example of Arab Spring to see how social media can catalyze political movements by facilitating communication and organization among dissidents in authoritarian regimes. In this context, DIDs can further empower individuals by enabling them to bypass state-controlled identification system and surveillance. This approach allows users to authenticate themselves and communicate over the Internet without revealing identifiable information to government surveillance or censorship apparatus. It can protect the anonymity and privacy of activists, allowing them to organize, share information, and mobilize without much risk of detection and repression. By decentralizing the control over identity verification, individuals can create a resilient network that is more difficult for authoritarian governments, potentially safeguarding the flow of information and enabling more effective organization of social and political movements against oppressive regimes. The fine line between security and privacy is crossed, leading to a society where every transaction is monitored under the guise of identity verification.

Security in DIDs refers to the technical measures, protocols, and mechanisms that ensure the integrity, authenticity, and confidentiality of identity data across decentralized networks. This encompasses the protection of identity records from unauthorized access, manipulation, or theft, and it includes the user of cryptographic techniques, secure channels for data transmission, and the robustness of blockchain or distributed ledger technology against the attack.

Privacy in DIDs pertains to the control and rights individuals have over their personal information within the DID ecosystem. It emphasizes the user's ability to manage their own identity, including what information they choose to disclose, to whom, and under what circumstances. Privacy in DIDs is about empowering users with control over their identity data, enabling selective disclosure, and ensuring that personal information is used in accordance with the individual's consent and preferences.

These contrasting scenarios highlight the importance of the ethical implementations of DID technologies. The direction toward a utopian or dystopian future largely depends on how these technologies are governed and regulated. Will they be used to empower individuals and foster democratic participation, or will they become tools for surveillance and control? The answer lies in the decisions made by technologists, policymakers, and society at large.

The Dark Side: Threats and Challenges in a Decentralized Ecosystem

In a decentralized ecosystem of advanced technologies, there is a dark side with significant threats and challenges, primarily related to cybersecurity and the exacerbation of the digital divide and inequality.

As we move toward a more decentralized ecosystem, powered by technologies like blockchain and AI, the cybersecurity landscape becomes increasingly complex and challenging. Decentralization, while offering advantages in terms of security and resilience against centralized attacks, also introduces new vulnerabilities. Cybercriminals could exploit weaknesses in decentralized networks, such as individual nodes or smart contracts, or could manipulate the identity verification algorithm leading to potential breaches. Additionally, the increasing sophistication of cyberattacks, including the use of AI for malicious purposes, poses a significant threat. These types of vulnerability demand constant vigilance and the development of advanced cybersecurity measures.

Another nontechnical challenge in a decentralized ecosystem is the widening of the digital divide and the resultant inequality. As cutting-edge technologies become a backbone of economic, social, and political systems, there is a risk that a certain segment of population may be left behind. Decentralization holds the promise of inclusive growth, but this can be realized only if concerted efforts are made to provide universal access to technology.

Navigating the Road Ahead in DIDs

As you navigate the road ahead in the realm of DIDs, you will find a complex landscape of challenges and opportunities, calling for concerted action from various stakeholders. One of the primary challenges lies in achieving widespread adoption and interoperability among diverse systems and jurisdictions. The decentralized nature of these identities requires the harmonization of standards and protocols across different platforms and countries, a task that involves significant collaboration and consensus-building. Another challenge is ensuring robust security against cyber threats.

Looking forward, there's a clear call to action for stakeholders such as governments, tech companies, and global organizations involved in the development and propagation of decentralized digital identities. Tech developers and innovators must continue to focus on enhancing the security and user-friendliness of these systems. Policymakers and regulatory authorities have the crucial task of crafting policies and standards that not only foster innovation in this space but also address privacy, security, and ethical concerns. There's also a need for a public-private partnership to drive the implementation of decentralized identity solutions in various sectors.

Education and advocacy play a vital role as well in raising awareness about the benefits and potential of decentralized identities among the general public and specific industries. By highlighting successful use cases and addressing misconceptions, stakeholders can build trust and acceptance of this new identity model.

Summary

This chapter explored the future of digital identities, moving beyond current blockchain technologies to envision future trends and innovations. It delved into how AI could become the custodian of our digital selves, offering personalized and secure identity management solutions. The chapter also speculated on the concept of interstellar identity in the context of space colonization and contemplated both utopian and dystopian scenarios for future societies shaped by digital identity technologies. This highlighted the potential for enhanced inclusivity and efficiency alongside concerns over privacy, surveillance, and social division. The chapter also discussed the dark side of digital identity, discussing challenges such as identity theft, fraud, and misuse of personal data. Finally, it emphasized the need for robust, ethical frameworks and international cooperation to ensure that the future of digital identities protects individual rights and fosters a more secure, equitable digital world.

Index

A

Account-based identities, 7, 8, 116
Actual identity, 122, 133
Aesthetic preferences, 52
AI-powered guardians, 46, 47
AI-powered identity, 46
AI-powered trust frameworks, 228
Amazon Web Service (AWS), 191
Artificial intelligence (AI), 3, 54, 192, 229
Asset tokenization, 89
Asymmetric key cryptography, 114
Augmented reality (AR), 176, 224
Authentication mechanism, 38, 42
Aviation industry, 127

B

Behavioral authentication, 42
Behavioral biometrics, 50, 51, 63, 68, 224
    gait recognition (*see* Gait recognition)
Behavioral identities, 12
Bertillon's system, 50
Biometric architecture, 68
Biometric authentication methods, 32, 42
Biometric data, 72
Biometric fusion, 228
Biometric identification, 230
Biometric identities, 11
Biometric raw image
    alignment, 70
    detection, 70
    normalization, 70

segmentation, 70
Biometrics, 11, 49, 131, 225
    role, 50
    types, 50
Biometrics systems, 49, 77–79
Biometric technologies, 53
Bitbond, 174
Blockchain, 82, 97, 131, 145
    asset tokenization, 89
    Bitcoin, 89
    capabilities, 89
    DID, 82
    digital identifiers, 82
    digital identities, 91
    shared ledger/distributed ledger, 90
    smart contracts, 88, 90
Blockchain-based Service Network
        (BSN), 201
Blockchain technology, 192, 226, 227, 234
Brave, 155

C

California Consumer Privacy Act
        (CCPA), 14
Centralized identities, 81, 92
Centralized platforms, 216
Centralized social networks, 141
Centralized systems, 82, 84
Chief financial officers (CFOs), 17
Claimed identity, 133
Cloud identity management (CIM), 22